Heroes
of the NFL

Ten inspiring biographical sketches of NFL heroes who overcame serious obstacles to become famous gridiron stars or coaches. The players include Raymond Berry, Frank Gifford, Lou Groza, Elroy Hirsch, Eddie LeBaron, Tommy McDonald, Lenny Moore, Allie Sherman, Emlen Tunnell and Willie Wood.

RANDOM HOUSE · New York

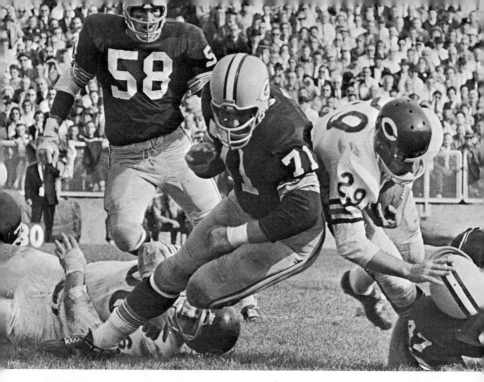

Heroes
of the NFL

by JACK HAND

Illustrated with Photographs
and Drawings by Fran Chauncy

Designed by Jennie R. Bush
Manufactured in the United States of America

This title was originally catalogued by the Library of Congress as follows:

Hand, Jack J   1912–
    Heroes of the NFL, by Jack Hand. Illustrated with photos. and drawings by Fran Chauncy. New York, Random House ₁1965₁
    183 p. illus., ports. 22 cm. (The Punt, pass, and kick library, 4)

1. National Football League. 2. Football—Biog.   I. Title.

GV939.A1H3   796.332640922   65—25456

Library of Congress   ₁66z4₁

Trade Ed.: ISBN: 0-394-80194-6   Lib. Ed.: ISBN: 0-394-90194-0

4/74

Introduction

In the precise meaning of the word, it is perhaps incorrect to call a football player a "hero." The word should be reserved for the men who stormed the heights at Iwo Jima, the resolute battalions who fought the Battle of the Bulge and all those who have performed an exceptional service for mankind.

But in the narrow frame of professional sports, a "hero" is a man who has performed an admirable part in a remarkable event.

Under that interpretation of the word, it seems fair to include such men as pint-sized Eddie Le-Baron and Tommy McDonald and near-sighted Raymond Berry, as well as Emlen Tunnell, Lenny Moore, Willie Wood, Frank Gifford, Elroy Hirsch, Lou Groza and Allie Sherman.

If their contributions to football have not been truly heroic, they certainly have performed in a manner that should provide an inspiration to young readers. The list is by no means complete. The rosters of National Football League teams are crammed with men who have overcome adversity whether it be size, injury, age, background or physical handicaps.

Hirsch and Gifford refused to give up and fought their way back after suffering critical injuries. McDonald and LeBaron were little men who became great players despite their size. Berry could not even see the big *E* on the eye charts, but he turned out to be one of the great pass receivers in pro football.

Sherman, a left-handed quarterback who was told to stick to handball, managed to secure a top coaching job in the NFL. Lenny Moore, written off as a "washed up" player, staged the comeback of the year and made his critics eat their words. Emlen Tunnell walked into the Giants' office undrafted, uninvited and unwanted and became the first man of his race to earn a full-time coaching job in the NFL. Lou Groza went on and on at an age when most men are ready to sit by the fire, reading their clippings. Willie Wood, a troubled youth, became an all-league defensive star and took on the job of working with boys in the District of Columbia.

If one boy who reads these stories is inspired to banish the word "quit" from his vocabulary, the retelling will have been worth-while.

Contents

Heroes
of the NFL

Elroy Hirsch

1

On a gloomy Monday morning in October, 1948, Elroy Hirsch sat hunched up in an easy chair. He was listening to the radio in his Chicago apartment. Every bone in his body ached, and sharp pains darted across his forehead.

Suddenly the telephone rang. Elroy turned down the radio and picked up the phone.

"Hirsch, stop whatever you are doing and get in bed," said the voice at the other end. "I just discovered that you have a fractured skull."

The call was from the doctor of the Chicago Rockets. He had just finished checking the x-rays taken Sunday night after Hirsch had been injured in an All-America Conference game with the Cleveland Browns.

Hirsch knew what it was to feel pain. The ligaments of his right knee were torn so badly that his old nickname—"Crazylegs"—sounded like a bad joke. And now, a fractured skull.

Was this the end of all his rosy dreams? Would it mean the finish of his career as a football player? Where would he go? What team would want him now?

All these thoughts filtered dully through Hirsch's aching head before he broke the bad news to his wife.

Days in the hospital stretched into weeks and more weeks. The crack over Elroy's right ear was dangerous. It healed slowly, oh so slowly. Though the doctor told him he would play football again, Elroy wasn't so sure.

Finally, it was February. Elroy was able to go downtown to a gymnasium and start light exercising. But something was wrong. The muscles were healthy; the tortured legs ached no more. But his coordination was off. That split-second timing was gone. He couldn't seem to catch a medicine ball, let alone a football. Maybe he would be better off to forget football and turn his attention to the small business he had started. Maybe he was through.

But Elroy had never been the kind to give up easily. A Hirsch never quit. He knew he was fighting the toughest battle of his life, and he wasn't going to let this latest setback lick him. He hadn't trained the muscles of his body for years to have his football career end like this. He wasn't going to throw away all those long, dreary hours of practice, practice and still more practice.

He remembered the day when he had first gone out for football in his home town of Wausau, Wisconsin. Actually track had always been his sport. In grade school he had been the anchor man on the relay team that won six consecutive city championships for Lincoln School.

But when Elroy appeared at football practice, the high-school coach took one look at the spindle-legged 120-pounder. Then kindly, but firmly, he said, "Hirsch, why don't you stick to track?"

Elroy dutifully turned in his uniform, but he went home determined to show the coach that he could play football as well as run. He would make Coach Brockmeyer see him as a football player.

He ran all the way home that night—two long miles—and the next night and the next night.

There was a clump of trees in a small park near his home. Elroy dodged in and out of the trees, developing the elusive moves that later won him the name of Crazylegs. He would skip and hop, crisscrossing his legs on the concrete sidewalk in front of his house, trying to land both feet on the lines that divided the walk into sections. He had always been fast but now he was getting shifty, too.

Body-building was part of the routine. In one year, Elroy gained 40 pounds. No longer was he a scraggly, anemic-looking kid. At 160 pounds he was on the way to manhood. When he reported for football the following September, nobody told him to go home and "stick to track." He was welcomed with open arms.

At Wausau High School Elroy first knew fame as a football player. He scored 85 points as a junior, and in his senior year he led the Wisconsin high-school conference with 110 points. Winfred Brockmeyer, the coach who had once told him to stick to track, became his closest friend. Years later, when Elroy married, he named his son Winfred Brockmeyer Hirsch.

After that spectacular high-school career, the local newspaper headlines screamed his praises, and it was "On to Wisconsin" for Elroy. Coach Harry Stuhldreher, who had been one of the im-

"Crazylegs" Hirsch

mortal Four Horsemen of Notre Dame, tried
Hirsch in an early game against Camp Grant.
Elroy ran 45 yards for a touchdown. In the game
against Notre Dame, he ran 33 yards for a touchdown that tied the score at 7–7. Against Ohio
State he gained more than 200 yards and even
threw a touchdown pass in a 17–7 upset victory.

Elroy's promising career at the University of
Wisconsin ended when he enlisted in the Marines
and was sent to Michigan as a V-12 officer candi-
date. Eligibility requirements had been relaxed
because of the war, and Elroy was able to play
football for Coach H. O. "Fritz" Crisler at the
University of Michigan. Old Crazylegs was on the
loose again until he tore a shoulder nerve while
throwing a block in the Indiana game.

Football, however, was not Elroy's only sport
in those days. As a basketball player he played on
the Michigan team that won the Big Ten championship. As a baseball player he struck out twelve
men in the game that won the Big Ten title for
Michigan. And that wasn't all. During the baseball season he also took time out to broad-jump
for the track team. In one meet he beat Buddy
Young of Illinois with a leap of 24 feet, 2¼ inches.

The professional baseball scouts were interested
in Hirsch, and the Chicago Cubs once asked him

to come to training camp. But the Marines still had Elroy and they weren't going to let him go. After a year at Camp LeJeune in North Carolina, Hirsch moved on to the Marine base at El Toro, California, where Dick Hanley was the football coach.

When the war ended, Elroy—by that time a married man—was under heavy pressure. He had retained his amateur status while playing for the Marines and he still had collegiate eligibility remaining at the University of Wisconsin, his original school. But because his original college class had been graduated, Elroy was also eligible for selection by the professional football teams. Both the Los Angeles Rams of the National Football League and the Chicago Rockets of the new All-America Conference were interested.

Hanley, Elroy's old coach at El Toro, was coaching the Chicago Rockets, so Hirsch decided to sign a contract with the new league.

Before he entered the ranks of the professionals, however, Elroy had one more collegiate game to play, this time as a member of the College All-Stars. Each August this team, made up of the previous season's best college players, plays the NFL champions in a charity game for the Chicago Tribune Fund at Soldier Field in Chicago.

In 1946, when Hirsch played with the All-Stars, the powerful, slick pros from the Los Angeles Rams were supposed to ramble over the collegians with ease. But the predictions were wrong. The football fans still talk about Crazylegs' play in that All-Star game. The first time he carried the ball he scooted 68 yards around the Rams' right end for a touchdown that broke a 0–0 tie. In the third quarter, after knocking down one of Bob Waterfield's passes, Elroy took a long pass from Otto Graham and completed a 62–yard scoring play. The All-Stars later added a safety and walked off the field with a 16–0 victory over the stunned professionals.

Hirsch probably made the one big mistake of his life when he chose the Chicago Rockets over the Rams. The Rockets were not much of a ball club. During Hirsch's three years with the team, up to his injury in 1948, the team won only seven games and lost thirty-eight. Hanley didn't last long, and other coaches followed.

Under such circumstances Elroy became disillusioned with pro football. The Rockets suffered defeat after defeat, as well as small crowds. And Elroy himself suffered a sore back, torn ligaments in his right knee and, finally, a fractured skull. But he stubbornly refused to give up the battle. It would have been easy for him to have drifted into coaching or some other business. But he was not convinced that he was finished as a football player. Day after day he could see his reflexes sharpening and his timing returning.

Ten months after the serious accident, Elroy was ready to give football another try. By 1949 his contract with the Rockets had expired. The All-America Conference was playing out its last season before merging with the National Football League. Earl "Curly" Lambeau wanted Hirsch for his Green Bay Packers, but the Rams still were interested and Elroy quickly accepted their offer.

Clark Shaughnessy was coaching the Rams in 1949. He knew Hirsch's case history, so before the club went to training camp Shaughnessy had Elroy running five miles a day to strengthen his leg muscles and toughen his body. He also devised a special head gear with extra padding around the right ear.

Shaughnessy's system called for a flanker who was placed wide to act as a decoy on pass plays. Elroy fitted the role. He did little running but he caught twenty-two passes and scored three touchdowns.

When Joe Stydahar replaced Shaughnessy as coach of the Rams in 1950, he decided to move Elroy to an end position after one of the regular

Ram ends was injured in an exhibition game. This was a brand-new position for Elroy. He had caught some passes as a flanker in 1949, but he didn't know the first thing about handling an opponent who would try to knock him off balance at the line of scrimmage. Elroy dropped the first three passes that came his way and was roughed up by the linebackers.

Red Hickey, end coach with the Rams and later head coach of the San Francisco Forty-Niners, urged that Elroy be given a real try at end. He took it upon himself to teach Hirsch the fine points of the position. What a teacher he must have been! By the end of 1950, Elroy had developed into a real end prospect; he had caught forty-two passes and scored seven touchdowns.

Like all successful ends, Hirsch was developing the art of running straight at a defensive back, then taking that quick step to the side which would enable him to break loose. He was also mastering all of the intricate pass patterns of the Rams' wide-open offense. By the end of the season he was becoming an expert at using his long, thin fingers for the fingertip catch.

In the long history of the National Football League, few ends have enjoyed the same sort of spectacular success experienced by Elroy in 1951.

With the expert coaching of Red Hickey,
Hirsch became one of the greatest ends of all time.

With Bob Waterfield and Norm Van Brocklin throwing both long and short passes, Hirsch grabbed seventeen touchdown passes. In doing so, he tied the record set by the great Don Hutson of Green Bay. Hirsch also gained 1,495 yards, thereby knocking Hutson's old yardage mark out of the record books.

To top it off, Elroy led the NFL in scoring with 102 points at a time when the league had such fine backs as Charley Trippi, Bill Dudley and Doak Walker running the ball.

Red Hickey, Elroy's teacher, always claimed that Hirsch was a better end than Hutson because he was more difficult to handle after he had caught the ball. This, of course, could be traced back to his change of pace.

Stydahar spoke often of Elroy's great ability to run with a football under his arm. "A lot of guys could run faster than Elroy," said Stydahar. "They probably would beat him in a race. But when you put a ball under their arms they would slow down. Elroy seemed to run faster with a ball than without one."

A fun-loving man with a sharp sense of humor, Elroy was known as the "holler guy" on the ball club. He had a reputation as the club comic, a man who could spread cheer in the most dreary situations.

Once the Rams were playing the Chicago Bears in the days when Ed Sprinkle, the Bears' 245-pound rough defensive end, was manhandling backs and ends. Sprinkle slammed Elroy to the ground with a particularly rugged tackle.

The quick-quipping Hirsch got up quickly, shook his finger at Sprinkle and said, "Flattery will get you nowhere, Ed."

After three years of high-school ball, two in college, two in the Marines and twelve as a professional, Elroy finally hung up the cleats in 1957 and moved into the Rams' front office. He still receives fan mail, however, when the 1953 movie *Crazylegs* or his 1954 production, *Unchained,* is shown on the Late Late Show of television.

In 1960 Elroy became general manager of the Rams when Pete Rozelle, who had been the general manager, moved up to become Commissioner of the National Football League. Hirsch had earned a fine reputation while he worked at spotting future professional prospects in the collegiate ranks.

During his playing career, Elroy suffered a fractured skull, torn knee cartilage, a lacerated cheek

and a fractured patella. And for six weeks he wore a wire brace on his arm. But still he will tell you that he owes everything he has to football. And any pro football man will tell you that the sport also owes a heavy debt to Elroy Hirsch.

For twenty-five years Elroy managed to play in some sort of a football game. He would probably still be playing at least one game a year if the University of Wisconsin hadn't finally eliminated its alumni game.

Elroy Hirsch is a man who never heard of the word *quit*—a man who made himself into a football player, then shrugged off pain to come back to the gridiron after long, dreary weeks in a hospital bed.

Two of the Ram's most famous stars moved into managerial positions in 1960. Elroy Hirsch (left) became general manager, and quarterback Bob Waterfield was named coach.

Allie Sherman

2

Allie Sherman rode the bench, just like the other second-stringers. When the coach looked his way he gripped his helmet tight and hoped. But it seemed that somebody else was always bigger, stronger, faster and better.

It was tough to sit on the sidelines and squirm while the regulars played the ball game, especially after all those grueling practice sessions. It was tough—but it paid off. The football lessons Allie learned during his days of picking up splinters on the bench helped him to become one of the most respected coaches in the National Football League.

Giant coach Allie Sherman.

As head coach of the New York football-playing Giants, Sherman stopped running second string, either in prestige or salary. He won three straight Eastern Conference championships in the NFL. And when age and injuries caught up with his team, he quietly began the job of rebuilding the Giants into another powerhouse.

The memory of those frustrating early years

have never completely left him. That is why Sherman is slow to give up on a rookie who is having trouble making the transition from college football to the professional game. It is also the reason why he is always ready to give a boy another chance. There is always the possibility that he may have overlooked some quality which could make the rookie a valuable member of the Giants.

When Sherman was a schoolboy in East New York, he was—by his own admission—one of the original "brown baggers." That is, he was one of the kids who used to pack a pastrami sandwich and a pickle in a brown paper bag and take off for a bleacher seat at the Polo Grounds, Ebbets Field or Yankee Stadium.

In Sherman's case it usually was the Polo Grounds because he was a football fan. In those days the Giants played their home games in the old ball park on Coogan's Bluff, which gave way to the wrecking crew after Shea Stadium was built.

"It wasn't that I was such a great Giant fan," said Sherman. "I don't remember rooting much for any team. I liked to watch the way the players moved and I tried to figure out just what they were trying to do. That fascinated me more than the score. Maybe it was then that I had my first thoughts about becoming a football coach."

During the early 1930s, the boys in the East New York neighborhood were more interested in baseball and basketball than in football, but Allie's main love was football. A wiry, little fellow who even at his full adult growth of five feet, ten inches would be considered a midget in basketball, Allie was too small for playground basketball.

Most of the other boys played basketball in the school yard all summer long, but Allie used to spend hours just throwing a football into a square cardboard box. He would play a game with himself to see how many times in succession he could hit it. Then he would turn his head away and quickly whirl and throw. He pretended that some of those big linemen he had watched at the Polo Grounds were chasing him.

At that time the main thing he wanted out of life was to play on the school team and become a star. He was so determined that he practiced every chance he got.

But Allie was destined never to become a high-school star or even a high-school player. When he went out for the team at Brooklyn Boys High School, the coach tried to tell him no as gently as possible.

"Son, you'd better try something you're better fitted for," he said to the scrawny 13-year-old freshman. "Try something like handball."

So Allie became a handball player. But he never gave up the idea of playing football. By the time he reached Brooklyn College, he made the team as a 125-pound blocking back in the old single-wing system.

Although he had been unable to get on the high-school squad, Allie had played football with the bigger boys in a rock-strewn lot near the sheds that housed the subway cars. While dodging the garbage and sharp rocks at old Tiger Field, he improved his game enough to attract the attention of the coach at Brooklyn College.

Brooklyn College was far from being a power among college football teams, but Allie was happy to be playing for any college anywhere.

"We didn't think so much about winning," he has said. "Just counting up first downs was a moral victory for us. . . . But we did beat City College."

By the time Brooklyn was beating City, Lou Oshins, the coach, had switched from the single wing to the new T formation.

In the old single wing, the quarterback was a blocking back. The ball was snapped from the

Allie Sherman as quarterback for Brooklyn College.

center to the deep back, known as the tailback, who then would run with the ball, hand off to another back or throw a pass.

In the T formation, now used by most college and all professional teams, the center merely hands the ball back to the quarterback, who lines up directly behind him. The quarterback may then hand off to the fullback or halfback, drop back to throw a pass, or run with the ball himself after faking a handoff on the so-called "keeper" play.

Obviously there was much work to be done in changing from the old single-wing system, with its accent on power plays and heavy blocking, to the quick-striking T formation, with its brush blocks and quick-opening plays.

Oshins decided that Sherman, who was working at a summer camp in the Catskill Mountains at the time, was the man for the job. The coach bought a textbook on the new formation, written by Clark Shaughnessy and George Halas. (Halas had introduced the T formation to the Chicago Bears after Shaughnessy had experienced great success with it at Stanford University.)

Oshins tore out the pages of his manual as he finished reading them and mailed them, a few at a time, to Sherman. Thus Allie learned the T through the mail. It was like learning to be an electrical engineer through a correspondence school.

This innovation occurred just before Sherman's junior year, and Brooklyn College enjoyed a measure of success with the new formation during his last two years. They crowned the first season with a victory over their traditional rival, City College.

By the time Sherman was ready to graduate from Brooklyn, he was an acknowledged master of the T formation. In those days he was known as "Biggie"—not because of his size but because of his admiration for Marshall "Biggie" Goldberg, the Pittsburgh star.

Despite his success at Brooklyn, Allie didn't have any pro clubs beating on his front door. But because the armed forces were calling up so many men to fight in World War II, football talent was getting scarce. The Philadelphia Eagles sent Allie a questionnaire. Earle "Greasy" Neale, coach of the merged Philadelphia–Pittsburgh Eagles, had heard about Sherman's ability to operate a T-formation team.

Since Roy Zimmerman was the Eagles' quarterback, there wasn't much for the number two man to do. Allie suffered through the ordeal of squad-cutting time, managing to stay out of Neale's way when the coach was in a bad mood.

Allie likes to tell a story about something that happened in 1943, during his first year with the Eagles. The Eagles were playing the Giants at Shibe Park in Philadelphia, where the club then played its home games. It was a tight contest and the Eagles held a 21–14 lead late in the game. When somebody intercepted a Giant pass on the Giants' 8-yard line, Neale jumped up and motioned to Sherman.

"Listen, kid," growled Greasy. "Get in there and sit on that lead. Whatever you do, don't throw any passes. Just send the fullback into the line and eat up the clock."

Allie was overcome at getting an opportunity to play. But why, he wondered, should he take a chance on handing off the ball to the fullback? He might fumble, or the fullback might mess up the play. Instead, Sherman decided to keep the ball himself. The Giants might chew him up, but it would be a glorious way to go.

Allie called a quarterback sneak while the big Giant line braced for the expected fullback plunge. Nobody expected to see 160-pound Allie, the smallest man on the field, go burrowing into that mountain of men. But he did. The Giants were so busy getting ready for the fullback rush that they never realized Sherman had the ball. He didn't stop pumping his short legs until he fell into the end zone.

Walter Mitty, the meek man of fiction who dreamed of great feats of daring, never topped this one. Here was Allie Sherman in his very first professional game, scoring a touchdown against the Giants.

"Sorry, Coach," said Allie to Neale when he came back to the bench. "I was just trying to kill the clock."

Greasy, for once, didn't know what to say. In a moment he came up with, "I guess, kid, you just didn't know your own strength."

The game between the Eagles and Giants was a night game played in Philadelphia. Sherman, however, still lived in Brooklyn. While waiting at the North Philadelphia station for the train home, he spotted Steve Owen, the Giant coach, and some of his players waiting for the same train. They didn't notice Sherman. Even in brightest daylight they probably wouldn't have recognized the scrawny 20-year-old lad in the raincoat.

Coach Owen was still ranting on to his men about the touchdown that Sherman had scored.

"You fellows ought to be ashamed," he said. "What a disgrace, getting beat by a bunch of humpty-dumpties like that. You were so terrible you even let that little half-pint from Brooklyn College score a touchdown."

The Giants made up for it the next time the two teams met. They ran up a 42–0 lead. Sherman, however, got into that game, too, and threw two touchdown passes in the final minutes.

But life was difficult for Allie in those early years with the Eagles. When Coach Neale barked at him, he lost confidence. He worried because he wasn't the number one quarterback. In his vivid imagination, every minor mistake became a major error.

"You'll be great because I yell at you," said Greasy. "That's why I keep after you all the time."

Sherman never did become a great quarterback. His main job during his stay with the Eagles was to run out the clock in tight situations. In 1948, after three years in Philadelphia, Sherman took a job coaching the Paterson Panthers in the American Association. While playing with the Eagles, he had also worked as coach at St. Joseph's Prep in Philadelphia.

Then, when Steve Owen decided to install the T formation at New York, he asked for help from his old friend, Greasy Neale.

"Get Sherman to help you," said Neale. "He knows more about the T than anybody I know.

He has the best brain in football."

Sherman accepted the offer at once. His first big assignment was to teach Charlie Conerly, who had been a tailback at Mississippi, the tricks of playing quarterback in the T formation. The job took a bit of doing, but Conerly eventually became one of the very best in NFL history.

"I don't know a thing about this," Owen had told Allie. "It's up to you to make it go."

Allie played only one game with the Giants, in 1949, and that really was supposed to be a joke. But once Sherman got into the game it was no gag. He turned in a masterful job.

The Giants were training at Saranac Lake, New York, at the time, and they had been invited to Ottawa to play the Rough Riders in an exhibition game. One-half of the game was to be played under Canadian rules; one-half under American rules.

"I wish I could play under their rules," Sherman said in camp. He was intrigued by the possibilities of performing on a field 110 yards long and 60 yards wide with an extra back to work with on a 12-man team.

Without saying anything to Allie, Owen told the equipment manager to pack Sherman's uniform when he shipped the team's gear to Ottawa. Then before the game Owen told Allie that he thought it would be a good idea for him to suit up. "You never can tell what is going to happen under these strange rules," Owen said.

Sherman put on his uniform and sat on the bench listening to the coach outline his strategy for the game. As the second quarter was about to start, Steve walked down the bench and stopped in front of Sherman.

"All right, Allie," he said. "Let's go. You're the quarterback."

Sherman clapped a helmet on his head and trotted onto the field. After a few plays the Giants' stuttering attack began to click. Allie was having a wonderful time out on the wide field, with an extra man to set up his forward and lateral passes. He drove the club down the field and scored a touchdown.

Since Sherman was not exactly in game condition at this stage of his career, Owen soon took pity on him and sent in another quarterback.

"Well done, my boy," said Stout Steve. "I've been around for a long time but you are the first man I ever saw take a team 108 yards for a touchdown."

Sherman spent four years with the Giants, directing the offense of a team that was a consistent challenger but never a champion.

When the Giants decided to make a coaching change in 1954 and promoted Jim Lee Howell to the job, Allie left for Canada. There he coached the Winnipeg Bombers from 1954 through 1956.

Jack and Well Mara, the owners of the Giants, brought Sherman back into the organization in 1957 as a talent scout in charge of personnel. At that time Vince Lombardi was directing Howell's offense. He was running it so capably, in fact, that he was tapped in 1959 to take the head coaching job at Green Bay, Wisconsin. There were reports that Vince wanted to take Sherman with him to coach the Green Bay Packer backs, but Allie remained with the Giants.

After two years as offensive coach under Howell, the big job suddenly opened up. Howell decided to retire, notifying the Maras of his intention prior to the start of the 1960 season.

It was no secret that the Mara brothers hoped to replace Howell with Lombardi. They had been intimately associated with him in the years preceding his departure for Green Bay. But Lombardi had just won the Western Conference championship with the Packers, and the people at Green

Coach Vince Lombardi.

Bay were in no mood to release him from the three years remaining on his five-year contract.

The Maras, however, had another excellent prospect right at hand. Allie Sherman was standing by, ready, willing and quite able to do the job. He proved fabulously successful. During his first year as head coach, the Giants drove to the Eastern Conference championship with Y. A. Tittle replacing Conerly at the controls. Not even the crushing 37–0 defeat suffered in the title game with the Packers, coached by Allie's old friend

Lombardi, could dim the glory of Sherman's great work in 1961.

The Giants won the Conference championship again in 1962, losing the play-off to the Packers on a bitter, windy afternoon at Yankee Stadium. In 1963 they won their third straight Eastern crown, only to fail once more in the championship game with the Chicago Bears when Tittle was crippled in the first half. In both 1961 and 1962 Sherman was voted "Coach of the Year" in the NFL.

Old age and injuries caught up with the Giants in 1964 and the team tumbled into the cellar. There were howls from the bleachers and some fans with short memories chanted "Good-by Allie, Good-by Allie," but the Maras paid no attention.

Sherman gamely set about the job of building a new football powerhouse. The Giants' last-place finish in 1964 gave them the number one choice in the annual draft of college players, and they followed through by signing such fine prospects as Tucker Frederickson, Ernie Koy and Bob Timberlake.

The "brown bagger" from East New York—the kid who was advised to take up handball instead of football—has come a long way. It's certain that he won't want to stop until he has done his best to add at least one NFL championship to his record.

Sherman makes a point to quarterback Y. A. Tittle and other Giant players during a 1964 workout.

Lou Groza

3

When the Cleveland Browns reported to their training camp at Hiram, Ohio, in July, 1964, a news story posed the question:

"Will Lou Groza, 40, be among the forty making the squad?"

Groza was the last of the "original Browns" who dated back to the club's formation by Paul Brown in 1946. And he was supposed to be facing the challenge of his life from young Dick Van Raaphorst, a bright-eyed rookie from Lou's alma mater, Ohio State.

Before the Browns broke camp, however, Van Raaphorst had been traded to the Dallas Cowboys. Once more Groza was in complete charge of all place-kicking duties with the Cleveland Browns.

Y. A. Tittle has hung up his uniform for the last time. Frank Gifford has retired. Gino Marchetti and Bill Pellington have told everybody they are finished. But Groza keeps on going although he passed his forty-first birthday on January 25, 1965.

When Lou played his first pro game for the old Cleveland Browns of the defunct All-America Conference in 1946, most of the 1965 rookies were still in the cradle. In fact, Jim Brown and Frank Ryan were only 10-year-old grade-school kids and Gary Collins, the other hero of the 1964 championship team, was a 6-year-old first-grader in Berryburg, Pennsylvania.

Some of the Browns call Groza "Methuselah." Others call him "Rip von Groza," "Pop" or "Gramps." When the boys are suiting up in the locker room, somebody may say, "Tell us, Lou. How good was Red Grange really?" Or "What was it like with the old Canton Bulldogs?" All these references to antiquity don't bother Lou a bit because he knows they are only fooling. The Browns have a deep respect for their dependable field-goal expert.

"I'll probably be around until they sweep me

out," Lou told reporters who were asking if he planned to retire. "I'll play as long as they want me. I never work on the principle of quitting."

That is the key of Groza's philosophy. He never works on the principle of quitting. It is a fine object lesson for all to consider when they feel like sulking or complaining because the breaks are going the wrong way.

When a veteran writer asked Groza, "When are you going to quit?" he got an answer that set him back on his heels.

"Don't worry about that," said Lou with a smile on his ruggedly handsome face. "When are *you* going to quit?"

Groza is the father of four children and a devoted family man. He is a vice-president of Insurance Counselors, Inc., a profitable agency in the Cleveland area and also owns a part interest in several dry-cleaning establishments in the area. Both he and Jim Houston have invested in Vince Costello's Boys' Camp at Millersburg, Ohio. These off-the-field activities will provide enough income to take care of the Groza brood if the club ever decides to peel the uniform off his back. During the summer of 1965 he shepherded a group of youngsters to Disneyland and also made an appearance at a sports festival at the World's Fair in

New York.

Lou isn't exactly the trim, sleek, whippet type of athlete. He was a burly 6-foot, 3-inch tackle in the years when he played on the offensive unit and did not confine his activity to kicking. Now he weighs approximately 250 pounds and has a slight alderman's paunch.

Since Lou's return from his one-year "retirement" in 1960, when he suffered a serious back injury, he has done little but kick. The one-time regular tackle on offense has appeared in only one regular play from scrimmage since 1959. In that one play in 1961, the Browns scored a touchdown. "Just shows what kind of a blocker I was," Groza said with a grin.

"I'm just a bottom-of-the-barrel player these days," said Groza. "They list me as an extra tackle or guard but they won't play me unless everybody else gets hurt."

But don't get the idea that Groza is any soft touch physically. In addition to doing the field-goal kicking for the Browns, he also handles the kickoff work. More times than not it is Groza who makes the tackle of the ball carrier on the return.

In a 1964 game Groza's nose was broken when he crashed into Pervis Atkins of Washington on a kickoff return. It was the first broken bone he had received in his nineteen-year career as a professional.

"Atkins was running at an angle and I just moved in to make the tackle when he cut," explained Groza. "The little bar on my helmet broke on contact and punctured the side of my nose."

Although Lou left the game with blood streaming down his face, he was back in action a few minutes later to kick a 35-yard field goal. The next week, broken nose and all, Lou kicked three field goals against the Detroit Lions at 38, 47 and 36 yards.

The 1964 championship game of the National Football League found Groza at his best. A strong wind whipped downfield at vast Cleveland Stadium as 79,544 fans huddled in the chill air and watched the Browns and favored Baltimore Colts battle through the first half in a scoreless tie.

A short punt into the wind by Tom Gilburg of the Colts gave the Browns possession near midfield. With fourth down and nine yards to go on the Colts' 37, the Browns called on "The Toe" to do the job. Groza calmly booted a 43-yard field goal that started the Browns on the way to a 27–0 triumph. Lou also kicked a 10-yard field goal in the fourth period and kicked the conversion point after all three Cleveland touchdowns, making a

total of nine points that he scored for the Browns in their startling victory.

"After Lou kicked that first field goal, inspiration set in," said Bob Gain, huge Cleveland defensive star. "A few points on a day like that give you momentum. After we got ten points they were running for cover."

It was quite a day for a man who wasn't even supposed to make the squad at training camp. The

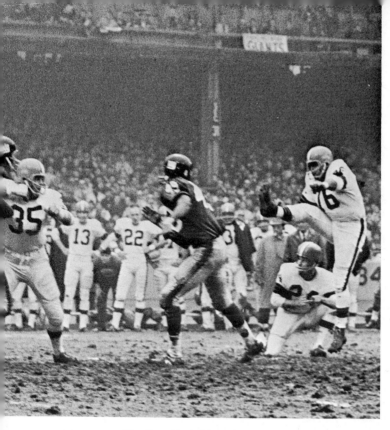

The New York Giants try unsuccessfully to block a Groza field-goal kick during the 1964 season.

nine points boosted his championship game total to a record 49 for eight games. His eight successful field goals out of fourteen attempts and his perfect record of twenty-five points after touchdown in twenty-five chances broke NFL title game records. The only other player to appear in as many as eight championship games is Andy Robustelli, who retired after the New York Giants finished the 1964 season.

"It was quite a thrill," said Groza. "This 1964 team came farther than any other team I ever played with. A lot of our boys matured during the season and hit their peak in the Baltimore game. We really were primed for that one."

But for his greatest thrills Groza still goes back to 1950—the first year in the NFL for the Browns. They had won four straight championships in the All-America Conference, which had merged with the NFL after the 1949 season. But they had to prove to the doubting experts that they were as good as the formidable NFL teams. The National Football League was a tough outfit with all the best players from the All-America Conference mixed in with the best from the NFL.

It seemed to the Browns that everybody was pointing at them, and there was a great deal of publicity about their first game. They played the Eagles in Philadelphia and beat them. Then they fought their way down the stretch into a tie with the New York Giants. In the play-off for the Division title they won 8–3 on two field goals and a safety.

Groza, of course, kicked the two field goals against the Giants.

"Then we had to play the Los Angeles Rams for the championship," said Groza. "We were losing 28–27 with just a few seconds left. We got

Lou Groza (top left) watches teammates carry Coach Paul Brown through the dressing room after the Browns won their fourth straight championship in the All-America Conference.

the ball with a long way to go, but Otto Graham brought us down close. Then it was up to me to kick the field goal from the 16. I made it and we won, 30–28. That really was a big thrill."

It was quite a moment for the man from Martins Ferry, Ohio, a mining town across the Ohio River from Wheeling, West Virginia. As a boy, he had been taught the first rudiments of kicking by his brother, Frank, who was the high-school star when Lou was still a grade-school youngster.

"When I was a freshman in high school, all I did was kick off and then go back on the bench," Groza said. "I used to be able to boot the ball into the end zone because I always did have good, strong legs."

As a sophomore, Groza became a regular tackle and kicked the extra points. Then in his junior year, when Doc Hartwig was coaching the club, he kicked his first field goal—a 25-yarder against Bellaire, Ohio.

Before Lou finished his schoolboy career at Martins Ferry, he had kicked four field goals. Gomer Jones, the former Ohio State All-America had been his coach during the senior year, and he was working very hard to get Groza to go to Ohio State.

But football wasn't Groza's only interest. In fact, at that time it may not even have been his foremost interest. For, in Groza's senior year, Martins Ferry won the state basketball crown, and Lou was named the most valuable player of the state tournament.

Athletic scholarship offers came from all sides, but Groza and his family finally narrowed the choice down to Ohio State and Notre Dame. The Irish lost. Knowing that he would soon be called up for military service, Groza chose to enter Ohio State in the fall of 1942. It was closer to his home.

Ernie Godfrey, then freshman coach at Ohio State, made the trip to Martins Ferry three times during the summer of 1942 to instruct Lou on the rudiments of field-goal kicking. The lessons continued during his freshman year at Ohio State, where Lou kicked three field goals for the frosh.

Before Groza could play a varsity game at Ohio, he went into the Army. It was a tough break for Ohio State, which had just brought in Paul Brown as football coach after his fabulous success at Massillon (Ohio) High School.

From 1943 through 1945, Lou served with the 96th Infantry Division and saw service in such faraway places as Hawaii, Leyte and Okinawa.

He played only one football game while in the

Army. That was at Bradley Tech in Peoria during the time he was stationed there.

Whenever Lou had a chance, whether he was at Leyte or Okinawa, he would set up a pair of makeshift goal posts and practice kicking a football, basketball or volleyball. The heavy army boots he wore may have been a factor in strengthening his legs for the long years of service ahead.

When it was time to leave the Army, Lou felt that his family could use a little financial assistance. He wanted to try playing professional football, so he wrote a letter to Paul Brown. At the time Brown was engaged in the job of putting together his first pro team at Cleveland. He answered immediately, and Lou joined the very first Cleveland Browns in 1946.

Before signing Groza to that first pro contract, however, Brown insisted that the young veteran agree to go back to Ohio State to finish his college education during the off seasons. Groza promised, and he attended school faithfully, year after year, making up the three and a half years he had missed. Eventually he received his degree in marketing, the foundation of his success in business.

"I would advise any boy to be sure he gets a college education," said Groza recently. "Football is fine but that degree really is important.

"As for the younger boys just starting out I would suggest that they concentrate on the fundamentals of football before they worry about complicated things like plays and formations. You have to crawl before you walk, and walk before you run. After you have learned the fundamentals, learn how to tackle and block at your own weight level. Of course, you always should have proper coaching."

The coaching that Godfrey gave Groza at Ohio State and the help he got from Paul Brown at Cleveland paid off. In his rookie year Lou became a sensation. As a member of the championship club, he led the All-America Conference with 84 points.

Groza actually set off a revolution in pro football with his accurate field-goal work. In the pre-World War II days, a field goal usually was the last thing that a team would try in a pinch. In 1941 the entire NFL made only 49 field goals in 118 attempts. In 1964 the NFL statistics show 214 successful field goals in 403 attempts.

The field-goal kicker has become as vital to a football team as the relief pitcher in baseball. No team can hope to compete for the championship if it does not have a place kicker capable of consistently kicking the ball between the goal posts from outside the 40-yard line.

When it is fourth down and long yardage inside the 50, most of the teams will send out a Lou Groza, Jim Bakken, Paul Hornung or Lou Michaels to go for three points.

Groza hit an all-time peak of efficiency in 1953 when he made good with 23 out of 26 field-goal attempts for an astonishing .885 percentage and led the NFL with 108 points. No wonder the Browns dominated the Eastern Conference in the period from 1950 through 1955.

When Groza's production dropped off to eight field goals in 1958 and only five in 1959, the Browns started looking for a replacement. In an off-season maneuver, they picked up Sam Baker to do their kicking. A training-camp injury left Groza with a sore back that pained him so badly he could hardly lift his leg. After a consultation with Coach Brown, he decided to retire and become a part-time coach and personnel advisor.

"I gave my back such a bad twist that I could hardly pick up my leg to walk, let alone kick," said Groza. "But it came around all right and I was ready to try again the next year."

Baker had not set the NFL on fire in 1960 and Groza was kicking the ball so consistently at training camp that he was reactivated in 1961. But he served only as a kicker, not as a tackle—except in the case of a dire emergency. Groza has been a part-time performer ever since.

Lou kicked 16 in 1961, 14 in 1962, 15 in 1963—the year he was second in scoring, with 85 points—and 22 out of 33 in 1964. He also converted 49 of 50 points after touchdowns in 1964, when he tied for second place with 115 points, barely losing the scoring title to Lenny Moore.

"Age doesn't have anything to do with kicking," Groza insisted. "The main thing is the timing. You must be relaxed, keep your head down and follow through. At first I used a tape measure to tell me the correct distance but the league outlawed the tape. Now it's almost automatic. You practice, practice and practice some more. I just try to do the best I can. Nobody ever will get to be perfect."

Because of his business connections, Lou does not get much chance to exercise during the off season. He does manage to squeeze in a handball game now and then. As the season approaches he concentrates on long walks to get his legs in condition.

His formula must be right. No man ever has scored as many points as "The Toe" in his pro career. His NFL total is 1,102. Add another 259

points from his four years in the AAC, and you get a dazzling total of 1,361 points.

In the years since 1946, Lou has scored just one touchdown. It came in 1950, the Browns' first year in the NFL.

The Browns were in Washington and Otto Graham had brought the team down to the Redskins' 25. In the huddle he called for the now-outlawed "tackle eligible" play.

Today only the ends and backs are eligible to receive forward passes. In those days the "tackle eligible" play called for the regular end to drop back off the line, leaving the tackle as the actual playing end.

With Groza as the eligible tackle, Graham threw a 25-yard pass to him for the touchdown.

"Funny thing," commented Groza. "The owners met a month later and changed the rules."

Lou "The Toe" Groza demonstrates his phenomenal kicking ability.

Raymond Berry

4

One of Raymond Berry's legs is shorter than the other. And without his glasses he can't even see the big *E* on the top line of the eye-test chart. In fact, when Berry plays football, he wears contact lenses. To guard against the possible aggravation of a chronic back condition, he also straps a canvas support around his waist.

But this same Raymond Berry is the star end of the Baltimore Colts. When Johnny Unitas drops back into the pocket and sets up for a pass, he automatically looks for Berry, his favorite target. The 1965 official National Football League Guide carries a line that reads:

Most passes caught: Raymond Berry, Baltimore, 506.

The active player whose total was closest to Berry's in the 1964 records was Pete Retzlaff of the Philadelphia Eagles with 346 passes caught, a score that was 160 behind Berry.

There is a lesson to be learned from Raymond Berry by every skinny little kid with glasses who thinks the cards are stacked against him. It is the old story of "try, try, try and keep right on trying." Success didn't come easily to this lean, near-sighted lad from Paris, Texas. But he made himself into a football star who never stopped trying to make himself a better player.

Night after night Berry would lug home the films of games played by the Baltimore Colts and games played by their next opponents. Hour after hour he would watch in silence while the action unfolded on the screen. When he saw a key move, he would stop the film and mark down the information on his clipboard. He noted which pass worked, which one failed—and why. He studied how his next Sunday's opponents had worked on him in their last game.

Some professional football players work at the job only from training camp in July until the end of the season. Others never stop trying to learn

The Colts' great end—Raymond Berry—pulls in a pass.

more. Berry belongs in the latter category. April finds Berry at Waco, Texas, teaching the ends of Baylor University the tricks he has learned over the years. In May he will be working out in Baltimore, running pass patterns and getting ready for the opening of camp in two more months.

Anyone who happens to stop at the Berry homestead in Baltimore in mid-spring may be in for a surprise. He may see the only husband-and-wife passing combination in football.

Sally, Raymond's attractive brunette wife, throws the football and Raymond does the catching. Sally isn't exactly a Johnny Unitas but she'll do until somebody invents an automatic football-passing machine. She can throw those quick 10- to 15-yard passes that have been Berry's trademark for more than ten years.

"Sally does a good job, Berry said recently. "We move around so much during the off season when I am coaching and filling speaking engagements that it isn't easy to find somebody to throw a football to me. Sally has been a big help. Of course, now that we have little Suzanne, she doesn't have so much time on her hands."

Berry prefers to be called Raymond, not Ray, just as many parents prefer their sons to be known as Michael, not Mike. "I never like to do anything halfway," he once explained. "My name is Raymond, not Ray."

Berry can be painfully honest. For years reporters had been writing stories in the Baltimore papers and elsewhere about the fact that one of his legs is shorter than the other. Berry always maintained that they were wrong. He thought people got a false impression from seeing him stretched out on a training table, where one leg would be turned a bit to the side, making it appear shorter.

For years he told everybody that story wasn't true. But then an osteopath friend measured him and discovered that one leg actually is about one-quarter of an inch shorter than the other. In 1964 he started to wear a heel lift for the first time.

The osteopath told him that the shortage might have resulted from an injury to his right knee. Or it could have come from the trouble he had with his lower back when he was still in high school. In any event, it is a very minute thing and doesn't seem to bother Berry in the least. But after trying to correct the story for years, he finally had to admit that the sports writers were right all the time.

Berry always has been near-sighted, but the condition was not so serious in his schoolboy days. When he played high-school football at Paris,

Texas, where his father was the coach of the team, Raymond wore glasses off the field. But during the games he got along as best he could without them. At Schriner Institute, a junior college in Kerrville, Texas, he followed the same practice. He was hoping to attract a football scholarship at a Southwest college.

When he went to Southern Methodist, he still didn't need any help for day games but he had trouble seeing the ball when the team played at night. Finally they fixed him up with some contact lenses for the four night games because his eyes were getting weaker.

When Baltimore drafted him, he tried wearing contact lenses in his rookie year (1955) but they weren't satisfactory. They gave him a great deal of trouble, in fact. But fortunately the experts kept working on him, trying to get contact lenses that would fit and stay in place when he was hit or shaken up in a football game. In 1956 an optometrist finally came up with the solution, and he has worn the lenses ever since.

The fans still tell stories about how games were stopped during Berry's rookie year while the players pawed about in the grass trying to find his contact lenses. But such a thing hasn't happened for years.

"I lost them in games several times that first year," said Berry. "But the only time I lost one in recent years was when I was recovering from a knee operation in 1961. We were playing the New York Giants in a pre-season game at Yale Bowl in New Haven and I was standing on the sidelines, playing catch. Something happened on the field and I turned my head just as the other fellow threw the ball. It hit me on the side of the head and knocked out the lens.

"Really, they are no handicap at all to me. If I didn't have contact lenses I would never be able to play pro football at all."

Raymond Berry, offensive end for the Colts.

Some people refer to Berry's unusual equipment as "gimmicks," but he doesn't agree. He has a logical explanation for the use of all these strange devices.

"The corset they talk about," said Berry, "really is a canvas sacroiliac support that I wear around my waist and hips. I have worn it since 1956. I have had trouble with my lower back off and on for years. During one off season I went down to see the team doctor at Southern Methodist. He recommended that I try this lightweight canvas support and it has worked out fine."

When Berry plays in Los Angeles and San Francisco, he wears a pair of rubber-framed sun goggles that make him look like a fugitive from Flash Gordon. Most people jump to the conclusion that he wears those special glasses in California because the sun is so much brighter out there. But Berry says that it really isn't that. Some stadiums, he explains, are laid out so that a player is looking into the sun at certain stages of the game. The Los Angeles Coliseum and the Kezar Stadium in San Francisco, for example, are so situated that in the third and fourth quarters he is looking directly into the sun when he goes downfield and then looks back toward the quarterback.

An inventive fellow with Berry's best interests

at heart designed a very dark set of sun glasses for him. The goggles snap on over his helmet with a rubber frame. Berry also wears his contact lenses, but the dark tint of the goggles neutralizes the glare of the sun. He has worn them since 1957.

Then there is the matter of the "silly putty" that he squeezes in his hand to reduce thumb and finger injuries. This substance, normally found in a youngster's toy box, is so unusual on a football field that Berry always has to explain its use.

"In my rookie year I had a lot of trouble with sprained fingers. Most ends have the same problem. It comes from trying to grab passes at odd angles or while knocked off balance. Our trainer, Ed Block, knew about my problem. He saw me sitting around, squeezing a tennis ball, trying to strengthen my fingers. Ed had done a lot of work in physical therapy at Kernan's Hospital for Crippled Children in Baltimore. He had used some silicone compound for the children with palsied hands. It strengthened the joints.

"Since I started squeezing that putty the most time I have lost is a day or two with a sprained finger. I used to be troubled for four or five weeks."

Berry also has tried surgical gloves to keep his hands from getting stiff on a bitterly cold day. In fact, the Colts' receivers and ball carriers were all set to wear the special gloves in the championship game at Cleveland in December, 1964. Finally, though, they decided against it.

Berry had worn the gloves frequently in practice, and they hadn't seemed to bother his sense of touch at all. He would have worn them against Cleveland, too, but he explained that the weather warmed up a little and the Colts decided they were not necessary.

Another gimmick that Berry has found very useful is a special backstop. He has rigged up a net with weights on the bottom that can be thrown over a goal post at one end of the field. It is very convenient when a player is learning to catch high passes. During such a practice the passer deliberately overthrows. The receiver tries his best to catch the ball but without a backstop of some kind he would spend all his time chasing the football.

Berry is an intensely religious person. "I do a great deal of speaking in the Maryland area and all over the country telling about my experiences since I became a Christian," he has explained. "Don Shinnick, one of our linebackers, helped me find my personal religion five years ago. It was in

Leaping high, Berry connects with a touchdown pass hurled by Johnny Unitas.

1960 that I got my first faith but it was a year before I realized the full significance of the change."

Berry also has great respect for the men who have coached him at Baltimore—Weeb Ewbank and Don Shula. "Weeb is a great man," he says. "I doubt if I would be with the Colts today if it had not been for him."

Baltimore drafted Berry as a "future" in 1954, but he did not join the club until 1955 because he still had a year of college play left at Southern Methodist.

"I just knew I was going to make it that first year," said Berry. "I was full of confidence. It was the next year when I wasn't so sure. I caught only thirteen passes in twelve games during that first season. I felt I was a borderline case when I went to camp the next July."

Berry had no reason to worry. During the ten years from 1955 through 1964 he caught 506 passes. He broke the all-time NFL record of 503 held by Billy Howton, now retired. In 1958, 1959 and 1960 he led the NFL in pass receptions and scored nine touchdowns in 1958, fourteen in 1959 and ten in 1960.

A knee injury suffered in a late 1960 game

against the San Francisco Forty-Niners threatened to end Berry's career in mid-stream. He underwent an operation for removal of cartilage from his right knee on August 5, 1961. Within two weeks he appeared at the Colts' practice field on crutches. By August 26 he had resumed practice. After missing the first three games of the regular season, he returned to action and finished with a total of 75 catches, the most of his career.

There was one disturbing phase to that 1961 season. Despite the 75 catches and 873 yards gained, Raymond did not score a single touchdown. When he scored only two in 1962 and only three in 1963, the fans began to say that he couldn't make the long cuts any more, that he no longer was the scoring threat that forced defenses into double coverage.

It took a 64-yard touchdown against the Detroit Lions late in 1963 and six touchdowns in 1964 to prove that Berry still was a threat, short or deep.

"I never was upset when the touchdowns dropped off," said Berry. "It did affect my pride a little when they said I couldn't go for the long ball, because it was not an accurate evaluation.

"But I never could understand all the fuss about scoring. When I scored it always was a pleasant surprise to me. I played end in high school and

Berry catches a pass good for a 25-yard gain
to the Green Bay 3-yard line.

college and never scored very much. I knew I was
playing the same as ever and was coming into the
games prepared to do my best. As long as we won,
what did it matter if I scored or somebody else did?

"A receiver can't have any greater blessing than
a great quarterback like John Unitas. I never have
seen anything to compare with him."

Berry spent most of the winter of 1964–65 trying
to explain to people what happened to the Baltimore Colts in the 1964 championship game with
the Cleveland Browns. In that game the Browns
upset the favored Colts and even shut out John

Unitas and company, 27–0.

"I don't really know what happened," said Berry. "It's something like trying to explain why you don't score as many touchdowns as you once did. I am thankful I have peace of mind about that game. I felt that I put the usual time and effort into preparation and got ready as best I could. You go out and try to execute your assignments. Sometimes you win. Sometimes you lose. I have no regrets. I was disappointed, of course, that we got beat, but I felt I did all I could."

The Colts had been in two previous championship games and had won them both from New York. But when they lost to Cleveland they discovered that losing a championship game is vastly different from losing one in the regular season. There is absolutely no chance to get even.

Berry, though, felt that the Cleveland team had earned its victory. "We weren't robbed," he said. "The Browns played a sound defensive game. They didn't double up on me as much as some people thought. In fact, that doubling up is a popular misconception. The defense guesses with you. Sometimes they put two defensive men on one player but they seldom do it over a long period because that leaves somebody else open. In that particular game, their linebacker, Galen Fiss,

A Detroit Lion tackles Raymond Berry—
but not until the Colt end has snagged
a pass for a 5-yard gain.

made some good moves. He would get in my way and force me to run a broken pattern. I remember one time John Unitas started to throw the ball and then let up when he saw Fiss forcing me to run where I wasn't supposed to be."

It was like Berry to give credit to the other fellow. He has been doing that all his life. He will practice all day and study all night to beat an opponent. But when it's over he'll shake the other man's hand and say, "Well done."

Raymond Berry's advice to young people could probably best be summed up in these words:

"Never do anything halfway."

Emlen Tunnell

5

"Mr. Tunnell to see Mr. Mara," the girl at the switchboard said to Tim Mara, founder and owner of the football-playing New York Giants. The time was a hot, summery day in 1948.

"Mister who? . . . Tunnell? Never heard of him," said Mara as though to dismiss the visitor. Then, changing his mind, he called out, "Oh, let him come in. What can we lose?"

From the moment that Emlen Tunnell walked into Mara's office, flashing his engaging smile, he established a special place for himself in the heart of the man who was most responsible for the success of the Giants.

Strolling in, undrafted, uninvited and unknown, Tunnell said, "Mr. Mara, I would like to try out for your football team. I think I can make the club." Immediately he made a tremendous impression on the elder Mara.

In 1948 the Giants did not have the high-powered, expensive scouting system that all professional teams now employ. It was quite possible that a young man could walk in off the street and turn out to be a real football player.

"Here, son. Fill out this form and we'll check up on you," said Mara, handing Tunnell a slip of paper. "Leave your address with the young lady at the desk."

It sounded like the old "don't call us, we'll call you" routine but Tunnell had faith in Mara. And his faith proved to be well placed, for the Giants' owner turned the information over to his sons, Wellington and Jack, who would eventually operate the club after their father died in 1959.

A check at the University of Iowa and at Toledo University brought fine reports on the young Negro halfback. Wellington and Jack made a date to meet Tunnell in Philadelphia at the old Broad Street downtown station of the Pennsylvania Railroad. In that unlikely place, Em signed his first professional football contract.

Tunnell was the first Negro to play with the Giants, whose roster was heavily laden with southern boys. It is to the everlasting credit of both Tunnell and the Giants that there never was any question of a race barrier. Within a week, Em was going to the movies with the rest of the team and had fitted into the picture as one of the gang.

"I never had any difficulties because of race when I was playing football," Tunnell said recently. "Everybody knew me back in Wayne [Pennsylvania] when I went to high school and played on the team. I never have had an unhappy day since I entered pro football with the Giants."

There were very few Negro players in the National Football League when Tunnell joined the Giants, though now there are outstanding Negro players on every pro club.

Little did the Giants realize what a prize they had landed on that August afternoon in 1948. And little did they dream that the same Emlen Tunnell would become, in 1965, the first full-time coach of his race in the National Football League. He was made an assistant defensive coach under Allie Sherman of the New York Giants.

All the odds indicated that Tunnell never should have played pro football. During his freshman year at Toledo, he suffered a broken neck and was told

never to play football again. For a year he wore a special neck brace. The Army and Navy rejected him as a physical risk, so he finally joined the Coast Guard. It was his football playing in the Coast Guard that led him to the University of Iowa.

When Tunnell came out of the service, a former Iowa tackle recommended him to Dr. Eddie Anderson, then coach at Iowa. The tackle had been impressed by Em's play in the Coast Guard.

"Jim Walker, one of my old boys, told me to get in touch with Tunnell," said Anderson. "He rated Em as one of the greatest prospects he ever had seen.

"I never saw a more intense competitor. In spite of that neck injury in Toledo, he was a vicious tackler. Nobody in this world could match him running back a punt. He easily could have been one of the great ends because he had the most remarkable pair of hands I ever saw. I was glad to recommend him to the Giants when the Maras called me."

At Iowa, in 1946, Tunnell was a halfback or tailback in the old single wing. Although he was a fine halfback, who could move the ball and score, Dr. Anderson wanted to restrict Tunnell to play-

Em Tunnell

ing on defense to stop the other team from scoring.

Determined to carry the ball on offense, Tunnell left Iowa and passed up his last year of college eligibility in order to cast his lot with the professionals. Before he decided to ask the Giants for a trial, he had made up his mind to try semi-pro football in the vicinity of his home town.

The Giants knew all about Tunnell's preference for playing offense long before he arrived at his first training camp. But Steve Owen was rebuilding a new club from the remnants of the sad 1947 team that had finished last in the Eastern Conference of the NFL, winning only two games. Long before Tunnell ever arrived at camp, the Giants had made a deal with Washington for the draft rights to Charlie Conerly of Mississippi. When they signed Conerly, despite a higher bid by Branch Rickey's Brooklyn Dodgers in the rival All-America Conference, Tunnell's chances as a running back were doomed.

A Giant publicity release at the time reported: "Since Conerly can pass and Tunnell throws well only underhand and on the bounce—Conerly got the job." But that was only one of many jobs up for grabs on the 1948 Giants. Owen had plans for Em on the defensive unit.

Tunnell was discouraged by his failure to win

the tailback post. He didn't realize that the shift to defense would be a tremendous break for him and the Giants. He discovered that defense in college football and defense in professional ball are entirely different. But it took him quite a time to learn his way around.

The Giant fans, impatient for a winner after the sorry season of 1947, made Tunnell's ears burn with boos and catcalls. When he raised his hand to call for a "fair catch" on a punt, they thought he just wanted to avoid being tackled. They didn't know that Owen had told him not to risk running with the ball, and had ordered him to signal a fair catch when a punt came his way.

Under the rules of football, when a defensive man signals "fair catch," the other team is not allowed to tackle him. However, the man catching the ball isn't allowed to run. Naturally, the fans wanted to see their man dash up the field after catching the ball.

Tunnell had trouble following the slick patterns of the professional passing attacks. Sammy Baugh of the Washington Redskins, one of the great passers in the history of the game, took advantage of Em's inexperience and completed several passes to receivers in the area Tunnell was supposed to be defending.

Thinking over that first year with the Giants many seasons later, Tunnell grinned and said, "I've got to love that man Steve Owen for taking chances on me. The way we were going he could have fired the whole lot of us."

Wellington Mara could recall one game in that first season in which Emlen did win his spurs. The Giants were playing Green Bay at Milwaukee in the old Fairgrounds Stadium.

"Em intercepted four passes that day," said Well. "If there ever was any doubt about his lust for tackling, it disappeared when he hit 'Indian Jack' Jacobs. Jacobs was rolling out, trying to throw, when Em hit him and sent the Packers' passer flying over the bench. They just rolled him under the bench. He was out cold."

The lessons of that frustrating first year paid off. In 1949 Tunnell intercepted 10 passes, gained 250 yards and scored 2 touchdowns. Discarding the "fair catch," Tunnell made up his mind never to field a punt without trying to run it back. Owen agreed to let him try. Em caught 26 punts and ran them back 315 yards in an eye-opening performance.

In 1949 Owen shifted from his old, outmoded single-wing A formation to try the new T formation with Conerly. Allie Sherman was brought in

Intercepting passes was one of Tunnell's specialties.

from the Paterson Panthers to teach Charlie the tricks of taking the ball directly from the center's hands and then dropping back into a pocket to pass. The Giants were on their way back as a winning team.

Owen devised his famed "umbrella" defense in 1950 with Tunnell as an integral part. Instead of the routine defense with the center dropped back behind the line and four defensive backs, Owen had the two ends drop back off the line to cover on pass plays. The entire defense sagged into a formation that resembled an upside-down umbrella. It looked something like this:

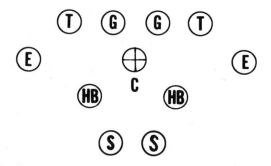

Tom Landry, later to become a defensive genius as a coach with the Giants and still later the head coach of the Dallas Cowboys, played one spoke of the umbrella as a halfback. Harmon Rowe was the other halfback. Otto Schnellbacher and Tunnell manned the safety spokes.

The new umbrella defense was raised for the first time when the Giants met Paul Brown's Cleveland Browns. They shut out the great Otto Graham, one of the finest passers in all football, 6–0. The smashing success of the umbrella in that game cured Tunnell of all ambitions to return to offense. From that day on, he couldn't have been pried away from defense.

In 1952 Tunnell, as a defensive back, managed to embarrass every offensive back in the NFL. The defense, of course, is supposed to stop the other fellow. Nobody expects the defense to move the ball. But Tunnell, a whirling speed merchant, was something special. He took daring chances and carried them out successfully.

In that one year Tunnell gained an unbelievable total of 921 yards on interceptions and kick returns—*all on defense*. The ground-gaining champion on offense that year was Deacon Dan Towler of the Los Angeles Rams, and he gained only 894 yards.

Gaining yardage for the Giants, Em watches out
for two possible Cleveland tacklers.

Only two offensive backs in the entire league
gained more yardage than Tunnell's 819 in 1953.
He set a record by running back 38 punts for 223
yards, and he also picked up 479 yards with kickoff returns and 117 yards on interceptions.

During his eleven years with the Giants, Tunnell played with two Conference champions. In
1956 he was on the Giant team that won the
league title by humbling the mighty Chicago

Bears, 47–7. In 1958 he was on the team that lost to the Baltimore Colts, 23–17, in the famous "sudden death" overtime contest that has been called the greatest football game ever played. It was the first time the championship game had ever ended in a tie. A so-called sudden-death extra period had to be played, with the first team to score a point winning the title. With the aid of Johnny Unitas' passes, Baltimore drove for a winning touchdown in the overtime play.

At this stage of Tunnell's playing career, Tom Landry was the Giants' defensive coach. Em played an "ad lib" defense, dashing hither and yon as the spirit moved him. He proved to be one of those gifted individuals who have a sixth sense that seems to tell them when a play is coming their way. It is spectacular when it works. When it fails, the results can be disastrous to the master plan.

Although Tunnell's instincts seldom failed him, his free-wheeling defensive moves did not fit in neatly with the strict patterns favored by Landry, who made a science of the game.

Consequently, when Vince Lombardi left the Giants in 1959 to become head coach at Green Bay, he was able to take Tunnell along with him for his defensive backfield by arranging a trade with the Giants.

Lombardi knew that the carefree Tunnell, an impish spirit with a fine sense of humor, would be the stabilizing influence he needed at Green Bay. He handed Emlen the same old number 45 he had worn at New York, where Vince had been an assistant in charge of offense under Head Coach Jim Lee Howell.

The clock finally caught up with Tunnell at the age of 35. He retired shortly after the Packers had thumped his old Giant mates, 37–0, in the 1961 championship game at frigid Green Bay.

"Em has been a lot of things to us," said Lombardi. "He was sort of an unofficial pastor, cheerleader and coach. I used to let him talk to the boys before a game when he was playing."

If a man had a recording of some of Tunnell's racy pre-game lectures, he could make a fortune.

"I ought to have been able to talk to them," said Em. "Some of those boys were almost young enough to be my sons."

When Tunnell finally did hang up the cleats, he insisted that he could still keep on making tackles until he was 50. "Your body may go," he said, "but your heart doesn't."

Actually, Tunnell hastened his own retirement by the fine job of coaching he did on his understudy, Willie Wood. When Wood was ready to handle the safety job, Emlen was out of work.

Norb Hecker, an assistant coach for the Packers at the time, recalled Tunnell's last year:

"When the opposition got inside our 15, we would put in Em and he would play like a linebacker. He could anticipate an offensive player's move just by watching for a tip-off. Then he really would nail him."

As it happened, Tunnell and Conerly retired at the same time. "When that kid Conerly decided to hang it up, I made up my mind, too," said Em.

The record book still shows Tunnell as the all-time champ with 1,282 yards gained on interceptions, 79 interceptions, 258 punts returned and 2,209 yards on punt runbacks. The 38 punt returns in 1953 are still a one-season record.

Em was a master at the daring trick of picking up a bouncing ball and dancing forward before anybody realized he had the ball. He became so proficient at this trick that the enemy went into spread or wide formations in order to get players downfield before he could get under motion.

After Tunnell retired he became a game scout for the Giants in 1962 and he also doubled as a college scout for both the Giants and Packers, with the special permission of Commissioner Pete Rozelle. As a game scout, it was Em's job to go ahead of the team and study next week's opponent. But when the Giants played the Packers in the championship game in 1962, Tunnell remained neutral. The Giants used films and did not bother to scout the Packers.

Tunnell became a full-time Giant scout in 1963, snipping his last link with the Packers. He would cover a college game on Friday night, another college game on Saturday afternoon and perhaps a third on Saturday night. And then on Sunday he would scout the Giants' opponent for the following week. That was Tunnell's busy schedule from September to January.

Each Monday morning he would be in the Giants' office with his charts and tables, plus a complete written report on the team he had watched Sunday afternoon.

Tunnell, a most likeable man, often shared the reports with reporters who were covering the Giants. Sometimes he horrified the conservative Sherman by predicting that the Giants would win their next game. Sherman never, never, never would make any predictions.

Laughs come easily with Tunnell. But he has a serious and sentimental side, too. No matter where he goes, he knows people. If he doesn't happen to find his friends at home, he starts telephoning. He has been known to talk on the phone for five hours in one day.

The Giants used to say that Tunnell had a pipe line to every source of information in football. He had his own little espionage network that proved invaluable in scouting Negro talent in the smaller colleges. For instance, there was the time that Emlen got a tip on a halfback from Philander Smith College.

"Even I had never heard of Philander Smith," said Tunnell. "I thought it was a pharmacy. But I went to take a look."

As a result the Packers wound up with Elijah Pitts. When Pitts, a Negro, seemed to be having trouble adjusting to Green Bay life, Tunnell took a hand. He went to Paul Hornung with the problem. After practice, Hornung came over to Pitts and said, "Come on with the gang. We're going to have some fun."

"Pitts went along," said Em. "After that he felt as if he belonged."

Tunnell always can feel that he belongs, no matter where he goes. As an assistant under Sherman he will be valuable for his understanding of player problems and his intimate relationship with the players.

The 1965 season marked Em Tunnell's debut
as an assistant coach for the Giants.

"I had two heroes in pro ball," said Tunnell. "One was Steve Owen, who took a chance with me. The other was Steve Van Buren of the Eagles. Not only was he the hardest runner I ever met, but he had so much integrity. I've tried hard to be that way, too."

Emlen Tunnell is a man who made it the hard way. As the first of his race to become a coach in the NFL, he deserves full credit for his own success. Unwanted, undrafted and unknown is no longer the story of "Emlen the Gremlin," the happiest man in pro football.

Eddie LeBaron

6

Every small boy who has shriveled at taunts of "pee wee" from the big fellows in the school yard can take heart from the story of little Eddie Le-Baron. He is the perfect example of a 5-foot, 7-inch, 165-pound half-pint who made good. Every skinny youngster with dreams of becoming a sports hero can find inspiration in the tale of this tiny Californian who became an All-America in college, a decorated Marine in the armed forces and a star professional quarterback in the National Football League.

Eddie LeBaron has a favorite story he tells about himself when he is called upon to make a speech. It goes like this:

"When I first started in the National Football League the program used to list me at five feet, nine inches and one hundred and seventy-five pounds. After a while they changed it to five feet, eight inches and one hundred and seventy. By the time I finally retired, they had me listed at five feet, seven inches and one hundred and sixty-four pounds. That must mean that over the years they have been cutting me down to my own size."

While Eddie was playing pro ball with the Washington Redskins and the Dallas Cowboys, he kept running into the same question week after week.

"How good a quarterback do you think you would have been if you had been six inches taller?"

Eddie had a stock answer:

"I don't know. I've never been any taller."

For eleven years little Eddie was David among the Goliaths of the NFL. How a little man like LeBaron could survive against pass rushers like six-foot-eight Doug Atkins of the Chicago Bears, six-foot-five, 300-pound Roger Brown of the Detroit Lions, six-foot-five, 275-pound Merlin Olsen of the Los Angeles Rams and six-foot-five, 295-pound Rosey Grier of the New York Giants and Rams was a mystery. How he could survive and pick out a target over the heads of those agile giants was still more difficult to understand.

Wasn't LeBaron overawed by those monsters of the NFL?

"I really didn't worry about those big men," said Eddie. "I think I got hit harder by smaller men who hit lower. Even in college, the other people always were bigger. They never worried me. If a man was good I respected him whether he was big or small. A lot of smaller and quicker men, like some of the linebackers, were tougher on me.

"Maybe being smaller actually helped me. It might have made me work harder to concentrate on making up for my size. I might not have gone so far if I had been big."

When Eddie ran out on the field, looking like a Cub Scout at a longshoremen's riot, the fans really took notice. It looked like a new version of the martyr versus the lions in the old Roman Coliseum. And the spectators enjoyed watching Eddie twist the lions' tails.

Every ancient joke about little men has been told about Eddie. The big linemen used to kid about losing him in the tall grass. Curly Lambeau, his coach with the Washington Redskins, is supposed to have moaned at first sight, "You mean that little fellow is supposed to play quarterback for us? We're really in trouble."

Tall tales of a tiny quarterback from Lodi in the rich San Joaquin Valley of California preceded Eddie's arrival at the College of the Pacific, where he formed a lasting friendship with the immortal Amos Alonzo Stagg. The stories told of a little man who could throw a football 70 yards and make the ball disappear before your very eyes.

Long before any high school, college or professional coach saw LeBaron, however, he was working with a football. His uncle, Jack Sims, a former football star at St. Mary's, had Eddie booting

LeBaron (right) poses with his college coach and longtime friend, Alonso Stagg.

spirals when he was only six. By the time he was ten, he could hit a receiver between the eyes at distances up to 50 yards. Although he was a 145-pound shrimp in high school, he once completed a 70-yard pass and scored 30 points in a game, plus drop-kicking the conversions.

There is a report that LeBaron thought of entering Stanford but was rebuffed by Marchy Schwartz, then the football coach at the university. "Go home and grow up a little," Schwartz is supposed to have told Eddie.

After trying the big school on the Pacific Coast, LeBaron realized that he would have to settle for a smaller college. He finally chose the College of the Pacific.

In his freshman year, LeBaron made the trip east to Evanston, Illinois, with the team. In 1946 freshmen were eligible to play college football at some of the smaller schools. This practice was a holdover from relaxed World War II regulations. The game was a dramatic event because Stagg, formerly the great coach at the University of Chicago, was returning to his old Big Ten territory with a new, virtually unknown team.

Northwestern University knew little about the College of the Pacific. It knew even less about young LeBaron, a reserve quarterback. When

Stagg thumbed Eddie into the game, the Big Ten giants had trouble restraining themselves.

"Watch out, Junior," a big Northwestern lineman yelled at Eddie. "Please take it easy on us."

LeBaron paid no attention. On the second play he dashed into his own end zone, intercepted a Northwestern pass and then flipped the ball laterally to a teammate, who converted the daring play into a 101-yard touchdown. Later in the game, Eddie threw a touchdown pass.

Instead of a 50–0 romp, Northwestern was glad to get out of the game with a 26–13 victory. Pappy Waldorf, the Northwestern coach, shook Stagg's hand and said, "That kid is the greatest I've seen in years—but who is he?"

Although Stagg soon gave way to Larry Siemering as coach at the College of the Pacific, LeBaron always recalled the Stagg era with deep feeling.

"I never thought much about Mr. Stagg's age at the time," he said. "When I came out for the team, his age was just something we took for granted. All of us knew about his great reputation at Chicago. He was a hard taskmaster on training rules, but he gave of himself and so did Mrs. Stagg.

Little Eddie LeBaron,
big star for the College of the Pacific.

I remember that she would take the uniforms home and sew them and sometimes clean them too.

"I've thought about it many times—the way Mr. Stagg was considered of no further help at Chicago and still went west and developed representative teams at Pacific. He bought some land near the college for ten thousand dollars. Later he donated the land to the college when it was worth over a million. He returned his salary many times over just in that one gift, to say nothing of turning out some pretty good football teams."

It was during Siemering's days of coaching at Pacific that LeBaron originated what is known in football as the "belly series." A quarterback thrusts the ball into the stomach of a halfback or fullback and runs with him a few steps. Then he may take back the ball and run with it, or pass, or let go of the ball and let the other back take it.

"One day we were running a play in practice," LeBaron has explained. "Out of the corner of my eye I saw the defensive end crashing in. I was just about to hand off the ball to our fullback for a crack at tackle. I still had my hands on the ball so I pulled it back and tossed it to another halfback who went wide around the end position left open by that crashing end.

"We made a regular series of plays from that maneuver at Pacific. And later, when I was with Washington and Joe Kuharich was coaching, we put in a whole system built around the belly series."

In one Pacific game against San Jose, Eddie faked the handoff and then passed the ball 40 yards for a 40-yard gain that would have set up a tying touchdown. But the fake was too good. The referee, confused by the sleight-of-hand work, blew the whistle and called the play dead when the fullback was tackled. Then when the referee found out the fullback didn't have the ball, he took both the down and the completion away from the Pacific team.

By the time LeBaron had been graduated from Pacific, the pro teams were very aware of his possibilities. His size, however, was against him. Washington drafted him number 10.

While the Redskins were negotiating with Eddie, Dick McCann, the Washington general manager, commented, "We'll probably sign Eddie. There isn't much difference between what he wants and what we can borrow."

LeBaron was finally able to work out a good deal for himself, but later he observed, "I think I'll go back to school and take a graduate course in persuasive English. After two days with George Marshall [the Washington owner] I think I can get an *A*."

In the 1950 All-Star game at Soldier Field in Chicago, LeBaron was the quarterback when the collegians upset the favored Philadelphia Eagles 17–7. Eddie had the Eagles running around frantically while he faked, ran and passed. A touchdown pass to Charlie Justice and a long gainer to Art Weiner contributed heavily to the collegians' victory.

After a couple of exhibition games with the Washington Redskins, Eddie was off to more important duty—service with the United States Marines in Korea. He spent nine months in Korea, seven of them in the front lines.

On June 26, 1951, there was a report from Korea that LeBaron had suffered an injury in action. In September of the same year he was recommended for a battlefield decoration. On May 24, 1952, at Quantico, LeBaron was awarded a letter of commendation for his heroism.

LeBaron never had much to say about his experiences in Korea. Years later when a reporter asked him if he ever feared for his safety on the football field, Eddie did tell of one serious battlefield incident.

After receiving a letter of commendation for heroism in Korea, LeBaron is congratulated by Lt. Gen. Clifton Cates.

"I never think about being hurt on a football field," he said. "The only time I ever thought about being hurt was in Korea, near the 'Punch Bowl.' I was carrying a wounded man in my arms when he was shot again. He died in my arms. I remember saying to myself, 'You may get it next.' Nobody will ever know who he was."

LeBaron bore the scars of two war wounds— fragments of shrapnel in his right shoulder and right leg—when he finally got around to resuming his football career at Washington after two years with the armed services. The strong arm that had been able to throw a football 70 yards in high school had been strained in a Marine track meet in Korea. His leg muscles, tightened by long, silent miles of marching through the Korean hills, did not respond readily to the requirements of football.

The Redskins counted on LeBaron to take the place of the great Sammy Baugh—if anyone could ever "take the place" of "Slingin' Sammy." The old Texan was nearing retirement and a new quarterback was badly needed. The only other Redskin quarterback was Harry Gilmer of Alabama. But Gilmer was a converted tailback and scarcely an expert at running a club from the T formation. A tailback in the old single-wing system took the long snap from center. A quarterback in the T stood right behind the center and took the ball directly from the center's hands. Before the T quarterback could throw a pass, he had to retreat six or seven yards into a pocket formed by his blockers.

During his first year Eddie divided the quarterback chores with Baugh. And when he pitched four touchdown passes against the New York

Giants, he made believers out of those who claimed he couldn't throw the "long ball." Although he won the support of the fans because of his size and his excellent faking during that rookie year of 1952, the Redskins still were not sure they had the right man for Baugh's successor.

After an ordinary season in 1953, LeBaron went to Canada for a year with the Calgary Stampeders, coached by his old Pacific mentor, Larry Siemering. George Marshall had picked up two highly publicized college quarterbacks, Al Dorow of Michigan State and Jack Scarbath of Maryland, and wanted to give them a trial with the Redskins. Eddie's "loan" to Canada lasted only one year. He was back at Washington in 1955.

Eddie has always been generous in his praise of Baugh for helping him over the rough spots in his early days as a pro. "Sammy gave me everything but his throwing arm," Eddie said with a laugh. "Actually, the big thing I learned from Sammy was that every player is an individual and what worked for Sammy wouldn't always work for me. I didn't learn technique from him, but he built up my confidence."

Baugh threw bullets. LeBaron couldn't get away with that type of passing if he wanted to. He had to loft the ball high over the heads of the onrushing defenders. They used to say he threw pop flies.

After the 1956 Pro Bowl game in which the pro all-stars of the two divisions compete, Pete Pihos of the Philadelphia Eagles had this to say about LeBaron:

"I can't even see the guy when I break down-field. I know he can't see me. But I go down and the ball is there. It is unbelievable."

In his years at Washington, LeBaron played under Curly Lambeau (1952–53), Joe Kuharich (1955–58) and Mike Nixon (1959). Lambeau, originally a doubter, became a believer. Kuharich built his offense around Eddie. Nixon called Eddie "the greatest ball handler I have seen and in the same class with Bobby Layne at picking apart a defense."

The runt who never was supposed to make it in pro ball had also been putting his free time to good use. During the off season he had been going to law school. In 1958 he received a degree in law at George Washington University, the same year in which he led the NFL in passing and again was voted Washington's most valuable player.

Admitted to the California bar in 1960, LeBaron joined a law firm in Midland, Texas, and an-nounced his retirement from football. The retire-

LeBaron scores a touchdown for the Redskins
against the Steelers in a 1952 game.

ment didn't stick. When the Redskins agreed to trade him to the new Dallas Cowboys, he decided to double at football and law. He explained that he could prepare his law work at night.

But Dallas had drafted a local hero, Don Meredith of Southern Methodist, as a quarterback. The Texas fans did not take kindly to the sight of LeBaron running the Cowboys while Meredith rode the bench. When Eddie ran out to play in 1960 there were boos in the Cotton Bowl. A record of 0–11–1 didn't help.

But the boos changed to cheers in 1961 when the Cowboys began to jell. Eddie was Coach Tom Landry's clutch quarterback. In his spare time he taught the tricks of the trade to young Meredith.

Larry Karl, the Cowboys' able publicist, said, "Eddie and Don were like twins in training camp. They roomed together. Eddie played golf with Don, taught him his ball-handling trickery and instructed him in the art of picking apart an enemy defense."

By 1962, Landry was using the shuttle system of quarterbacks—Meredith and LeBaron, back and forth. Meredith was learning, but the Cowboys still used LeBaron for the big plays against the toughest teams—especially the Giants.

Determined to make Meredith the number one

boy, Landry dropped LeBaron to the role of a sub-
stitute in 1963. He was used sparingly while Meredith took charge. At the end of the 1963 season,
LeBaron announced his retirement. He took a job
as executive vice-president of a cement company
in Reno, Nevada.

When the Cowboys ran into a series of injuries
in the 1964 season and Meredith was hobbling on
a bad knee, LeBaron gamely offered to come out
of retirement.

"I run a mile a day," he said in Reno. "My legs
are okay. I would go all out for it. It would be a
matter of getting my arm in shape."

As it turned out, Dallas was able to come up
with another quarterback and LeBaron was not
needed. Old number 14 would have to confine his
actions to the business world.

But the success of Eddie LeBaron is a heart-
warming tale of a man who triumphed over physical deficiencies. A story of a "pee wee" who became a giant in the NFL.

Frank Gifford

7

It was the middle of March in 1962. Casey Stengel was struggling with his first Met baseball team. Arnold Palmer, the golfer, was gunning for revenge in the Masters. Eddie Arcaro, the jockey, had just retired. In the Giants' office at Columbus Circle, Allie Sherman was looking at football movies, trying to unravel the mystery of his team's 37–0 beating by Green Bay in the championship game.

Frank Gifford, a handsome radio sports commentator, walked into Sherman's office and closed the door behind him.

"Allie, I want to play football again," he said. "What do you think?"

A startled Sherman, jolted out of his daydreams, sat up straight in his chair. "Say that again, Frank," Allie said.

"I want to play football again."

Sherman swung the door open and, grabbing Gifford by the arm, walked down the short hallway to the office of Wellington Mara, who was talking with his brother, Jack, the other co-owner of the New York Giants.

"Frank wants to play football again," said Allie.

"Wonderful," said the two Maras. "But are you sure?"

"I never could be more sure of anything. I've had all the tests. I'm tired of watching. I'd like to play a couple of more seasons, maybe three. I'll have to see for myself."

Frank Gifford, the handsome radio man, was, of course, the same Frank Gifford who had been the star halfback of the Giants from 1952 to 1960. He was also the same matinee-idol type who had wowed the spectators at the University of Southern California football games during his days as an All-America.

It was also the same Frank Gifford who had been carried off the field at Yankee Stadium on November 20, 1960, suffering from a severe head injury after he had been hit by Chuck Bednarik

Handsome Frank Gifford, the Giants' star halfback.

of the Philadelphia Eagles on a crashing blind-side tackle. The memory of that November afternoon, and the fearful moments before Gifford regained consciousness at St. Elizabeth's Hospital, must have been uppermost in the minds of the little group gathered in the Maras' office, listening to Frank Gifford's proposal to return to active playing.

Wave after wave of boos had rolled out of the deep caverns of Yankee Stadium when Bednarik raised his arm in triumph over the stricken Gifford. But, as Bednarik explained later, he wasn't aware that Gifford had been injured. He was leaping with joy because the ball had been fumbled and the Eagles' recovery practically assured Philadelphia of the 1960 Eastern Conference title.

"I pranced over him," said Bednarik, "but I didn't know he was hurt. The clock was running out. It was our first win in eight or nine years in New York and my first championship."

When he realized the implications of his action, Bednarik was eager to make amends. "We came together full force," he explained. "I can't regret playing that way, but it is a shame he was hurt. I never want to see anybody hurt."

The films showed that Bednarik was behind the play. After Gifford caught the ball and cut sharply

Chuck Bednarik (60) crashes into Frank Gifford (16) in the famous tackle that knocked the Giant halfback out of the game.

to his right, he ran into the hulking linebacker. The collision was a surprise to both men.

"I remember nothing about the tackle," Gifford said later. "After looking at the films I would say it was bad timing on my part. Normally when you catch a ball you are in balance and are able to control yourself. But I was off balance when Bednarik hit me. He hit me hard but I have been hit like that before by many other players. It is all part of the game."

During the anxious hours before Gifford's injury was diagnosed as a severe brain concussion, and not the fractured skull that had been feared, Bednarik sent wires and letters to the hospital.

"I didn't answer any of them for a week," Gifford later confided. "Know why? The Giants were playing the Eagles again the following Sunday and I wanted him to stay subdued. But, after they beat us again, I thanked him profusely for his wires. Chuck was just doing his job.

"He and I have been friends for years and we still are friends. When we meet he asks me about my family and I ask him about his. We never even mention the incident. As far as I am concerned, it was just an unfortunate accident and it has been forgotten."

Although Gifford had proceeded to wipe the incident out of his mind, the Giants remained very much aware of it. When Frank was released from the hospital with the clearance of Dr. Francis Sweeny, the club physician, the Maras insisted on taking no chances. They sent Gifford to a brain specialist for extra tests. In fact, Frank had undergone another series of tests shortly before that March day in 1962 when he walked into Sherman's office announcing that he wanted to play football again.

During his one-year "retirement" Frank had kept busy as a sports commentator for WCBS, the New York affiliate of the Columbia Broadcasting System. On Sunday afternoons he worked for the

Giants as a scout. It was Gifford's job to travel to the city where the Giants' next opponent was playing and then report back to the coach with a detailed written and verbal analysis of the game.

"I didn't retire because of the crack on the head," said Gifford in 1961. "There was a lot of gossip that the doctors didn't want me to play. That wasn't true. They said I could play. But I just decided that nine years as a halfback in this league are enough for any man."

But a year on the sidelines, squirming while the Giants went through the tense moments of another championship season, was too much for Gifford. Matters finally reached a head, in his own mind, when he sat in the stands at Green Bay on New Year's Eve, 1961, and watched the Giants lose the title game to the Packers by a score of 37–0.

"What am I doing up here?" Gifford asked himself. "I should be down there with them. I'm no scout. I'm a football player." Although he didn't tell the Maras or Allie Sherman, Gifford already had decided to try for a comeback in 1962.

During the 1962 season, Gifford often talked about his year on the sidelines. He said that what he missed most of all was not being an active part of it. He missed the feeling of belonging, of being one of the guys.

"Look, I wouldn't be coming back," he said, "if I was worried about the injury. I've had all the tests. I don't think I'm taking any gamble. I have three kids. It wouldn't be fair to my family if there was any risk."

Gifford rejected the idea of people thinking that he had been knocked out of pro football. "I get more excitement in one day of playing football," he said, "than most people get in a lifetime. I know you hear professional athletes saying they're going to quit when they get a good job. Well, I had

Having made a successful comeback, Gifford (third from left) poses proudly with (left to right) Y. A. Tittle, Alex Webster and Phil King a few days before the 1964 season opener.

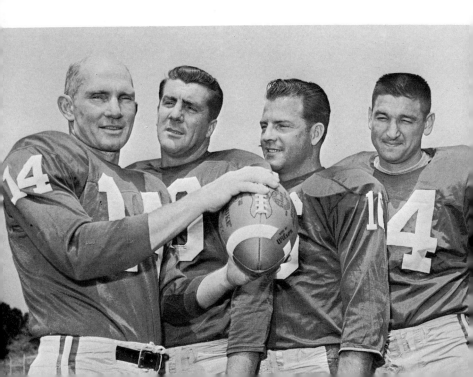

a good job and I still came back. Call it pride, ego or whatever you like. I just had to try again."

Gifford had always had to fight for everything he got. During his freshman year at the high school in Bakersfield, California, his first coach, Homer Beatty, had shooed him away to the lightweight squad. He was the third-string end on the lightweights. The following year, 1945, he was the number two end on the varsity. Then, when the first-string quarterback was injured in an auto accident in 1946, Gifford was drafted into service at that position. Coach Beatty, who was to have an important influence on Gifford throughout his football career, used him as a tailback in the single-wing system during Frank's senior year, 1947.

After a year at Bakersfield Junior College under the coaching of Jack Frost, Gifford moved up to the University of Southern California. Jeff Cravath, the coach, found a place for him as a defensive safety man and place kicker.

In 1950, his junior year, Gifford begged for a chance to play quarterback against Washington State when USC trailed, 20–0. He got his chance and pulled the Trojans up into a 20–20 tie.

Jesse Hill, who had succeeded Cravath as head coach, described Gifford as being "every inch an All American" during his senior year. He ended a

Halfback Frank Gifford makes a short gain for USC.

long California winning streak with a 69-yard touchdown run and gained 155 yards rushing in a powerful performance. Against Notre Dame he played the entire sixty minutes.

Gifford and his beautiful wife, Maxine, were invited to a Hollywood mansion by a scout for the Edmonton club of the Canadian League. The scout piled twenty-five $100 bills on the table and offered him a guarantee of $12,000 to play Canadian ball. Gifford turned it down and accepted an offer from the Giants.

As a rookie, in 1952, Gifford got a chance on offense when Kyle Rote was injured. But Coach Steve Owen, desperate for help, also used him on defense. After Frank did a fine job of covering Green Bay's Billy Howton, the Giants used him as a two-way man in 1953, Owen's last year.

When Jim Lee Howell took over as Giant coach in 1954, he called Gifford aside. "You are the man who is going to make our new offense click. No more two-way play for you. From now on you are our left halfback."

In 1955 Gifford turned down another Canadian offer, this time from Harry Sonshine of the Toronto Argos. And in 1956 he was named the Most Valuable Player in the NFL when he carried the ball for 819 yards running and also nabbed 51 passes for 603 additional yards. The Giants won the league championship in 1956, whipping the Bears, 47–7, in the title game.

During those great years from 1956 through 1959, Gifford was one of the inspirational leaders of the Giants, along with Charlie Conerly, Alex Webster and Kyle Rote. In 1959 he decided he wanted to try for the quarterback job. The Giants' owners, however, made a deal for George Shaw, so Gifford went back to his old halfback position.

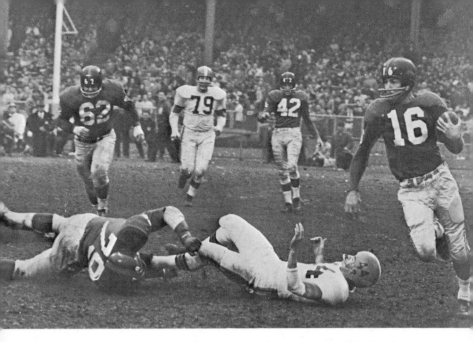

Gifford scores his second touchdown against Cleveland during the Eastern Division playoff in 1959.

This was the brilliant career Frank Gifford had to live up to when he reported to the Giants' training camp to start his comeback in 1962. Things were not the same, however. There was a new passer. Y. A. Tittle had taken over from Charlie Conerly, and it took time for Frank to get used to the change.

"Chuck would let the ball go and lead you with more of a soft pass," said Gifford. "Y. A. liked to hold the ball longer and then slam it at you. The ball was heavier and harder to handle. Most of all, Y. A. had to get used to my moves. Del Shofner and I have different moves. It took some time for us to click."

The Giants' first scrimmage at their training camp at Fairfield University, Connecticut, convinced Gifford that his comeback would not be easy. On the first play from scrimmage, he ran the wrong way.

"What happened?" asked Kyle Rote, his old pal, who had retired to coaching duty. "You've had a whole year to figure out which way the play goes."

Gifford grinned and dug in harder than ever. But he was having trouble getting his timing back. To make matters worse Frank hurt his back in his first practice scrimmage. After the first exhibition game with Los Angeles, Sherman decided to make a change.

The Giants' coach had hoped to install a man-in-motion offense, using Jim Podoley on the flank. But Podoley had lost too much of his speed because of operations on both knees. The new offense was junked, and Sherman returned to the familiar "three end" system used by most pro clubs. He needed a flankerback badly, and the more he thought about Gifford the more he became convinced that he should move Frank outside to the position vacated when Kyle Rote retired.

In his first game at this strange position, Gifford dropped three passes. It was only an exhibition game against the Eagles at Palmer Stadium in Princeton, but the failures were enough to make Gifford start to wonder about himself.

"I never felt lower than after that game in Princeton," he said. "I couldn't hold a pass. But Allie saved me. He told me everyone else had confidence in me so that all I had to do was work on my timing and get ready. After Allie shifted me to flankerback, though, I really had to wonder if he had as much faith in me as he said."

It was a difficult transition period for Gifford. As the left halfback he had been used to running the ball into the thick of the defense. When he caught a pass, he usually received it over his left shoulder. Now he was stationed way out wide, away from the heavy traffic, usually outside the right end. When he broke downfield and cut toward the sidelines, he usually was taking the ball over his right shoulder. Though that may not appear difficult, Gifford was uncomfortable running the opposite way. As a result he dropped more passes than he had in his previous job. The flankerback almost never runs with the ball. He is really a "third end" on the attack.

As a running back, Gifford had to contend with the linebackers most of the time, once he slid through the big defensive linemen. As the flanker, he had to work on the fleet defensive halfbacks.

"You go down into the defensive man and you make your move," explained Gifford. "If the fake and cut are good enough, you break away from him and you are in the open. Then you wait for Tittle to throw it to you."

At the beginning Y. A. appeared to favor Shofner in a tough situation.

"I didn't know what Frank could do," said Tittle. "So with long yardage I would go for the man I knew—Shofner. Now that I know what he does, I go to Frank."

Gifford's comeback came into full bloom in the Pittsburgh game early in October of 1962 when he made three terrific catches and scored a touchdown.

"I had my problems," Gifford admitted. "When you are trying to catch a ball while running to your right, it spins differently and hits the hands in an unfamiliar position. At first I wasn't sure how far to split out and how to handle the defense. After a while it began to come to me.

"Wasn't it Yogi Berra who once said, 'How can a guy hit and think at the same time?' I had the same problem. But by the end of that 1962 season I began to feel comfortable again."

Gifford caught 39 passes for 796 yards and

scored seven touchdowns in his 1962 comeback season. One of the scores came on a run when he cut back from the flanker position and took a handoff up the middle just as in the old days.

The 1963 season, however, started out badly for him. When the Giants went out to Cleveland and thumped the Browns 33–6 in a tremendous game, Gifford got into the game for only a few plays. Aaron Thomas, his replacement, had such a fine day that the papers began writing Frank's football obituary.

"It's happened to others and I was wondering if it was happening to me," said Gifford. "Aaron played a great game and we won, but I didn't have any part in it."

Gifford's obit went into the ash can when he bounced back with a sensational game against St. Louis. They still talk about a fingertip catch he made to snare a 41-yard touchdown pass from Tittle.

When the Giants came down to the last game of the 1963 season in need of a win over Pittsburgh to clinch a third straight Eastern Conference title, it was Gifford again who made the big play.

During the 1963 Eastern Conference championship game against the Steelers, Gifford snares a pass from quarterback Y. A. Tittle.

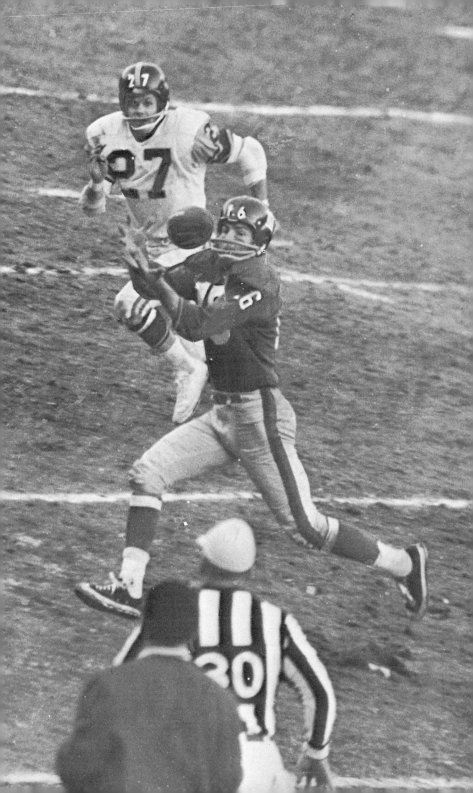

The Giants led, 16–10, in the third period, but they were in a third-down-and-eight-to-go situation on their own 24. If they had to give up the ball, the Steelers would be in position to pull the game out.

Gifford broke to his left and Tittle threw the ball low. Frank reached low to the ground and caught the hard pass with one hand for the play that was the key to victory.

"It was the biggest catch I ever made," said Frank. "All I was trying to do was to bat the ball up in the air and it stuck in my hand. I didn't think I would get it either."

The Giants went on to win the game and the Eastern championship. But then they had to bow to the Chicago Bears on a bitter, cold day at Wrigley Field.

After the harrowing season of 1964, when the Giants plummeted into the cellar of the Eastern Conference, Gifford decided he had had enough. With his thirty-fifth birthday closing in on him, Frank took over the job of doing the color work on the telecasts of Giant games in addition to his regular work as director of sports for New York's CBS outlet.

When he stepped down, Gifford held several club records. He had scored more points (484) than any Giant, caught more passes (387), gained the most yards with his catches (5,434) and scored the most touchdowns (78).

After 12 grueling years in the National Football League, Gifford still weighed approximately 195 pounds, the same weight he brought into the Giants' camp in 1952 when he was the club's number one draft choice. His comeback in a new, more difficult position crowned a fantastic career.

The Giants had no doubts about Frank Gifford's carving out a successful career in television, too. He has proved himself an All-American all the way.

Willie Wood

8

Willie Wood used to stand on the street corners in Washington, D.C., "hanging out with the guys." They called themselves the Tagalongs. None of them had much money. They didn't have much fun either.

At night they would play cards under a street light or listen to a ball game on the radio. Some nights they would get into a fight. It might be one against one—or one gang against another if the 12th Street Boys were feeling edgy. Mostly they just stood around on the sidewalk or loafed in front of the candy store, waiting for something to happen.

Any police officer knows that gangs of boys with nothing to do can get into serious trouble. Petty little incidents grow into serious violations. Repeated friendly warnings, if ignored, can lead to police records. The border line is thin between the boy on the street corner and the juvenile delinquent. In a poverty area like the Northwest District of Washington in the early 1950s anything can happen. And it usually isn't good.

Fortunately for Willie Wood, the right things happened to him. A boys' club opened up just a block from his house. The supervisor, Jabbo Kenner, took a special interest in Willie and treated him like a son. Sports became a new way of life for the boy.

Football, baseball, basketball, volleyball and boxing took the place of loitering, card playing and street fighting. Willie went on to Armstrong High School in Washington, Coalinga Junior College in California, the University of Southern California and finally to the Green Bay Packers of the National Football League.

The transition from a nobody to a somebody was rapid. But Willie has not forgotten those long, hot summer nights under the street lights in the old number two district.

At Southern California, Wood first decided to

concentrate on a physical education course, with the idea of becoming a coach. He soon gave it up, however, discouraged by his early bouts with science. Instead, he switched to a major in juvenile control, a subject connected with sociology.

It will be some time, though, before Willie Wood can devote his full attention to social work, for Vince Lombardi and the Green Bay Packers consider him a vital part of their fine defensive unit. As the "free safety" in the Packers' secondary, Willie plays a sort of roving centerfield, à la Willie Mays.

In the professional football defense used by most of the teams, the right safety is known as the "free safety." Most teams line up with more backs to the right than to the left. This puts heavy pressure on the left safety, who must handle the big right ends so numerous in the NFL. The *right* safety, on the other hand, usually has more freedom to roam, more opportunities to intercept passes when he comes to the aid of the other defensive backs. Some pro teams shift their safety men, depending on the other club's offense, but the Packers always leave Willie on the right side.

Now that Willie Wood has been voted an All-League defensive back, it is difficult to understand how he was passed up in the professional draft. He

wrote letters to all the NFL teams after nobody drafted him, and eventually he signed with Green Bay as a free agent. A free agent is a man who is actually trying out on his own with no bonus payment or encumbering contract to influence the opinion of the coaching staff in his favor.

When Willie came out of Armstrong High School with a so-so scholastic record, he originally planned to enter the University of Idaho, because there were many Washington, D.C., boys playing football at that school. But the coach who was going to bring Wood to Idaho was fired, and Willie had to make other arrangements.

"My grades weren't too hot," said Willie. "My high school average was C-minus so I decided I'd better go to junior college. I could have had a football scholarship at Southern California, but my grades weren't good enough. I also was thinking of the University of Iowa because a buddy of mine was playing there.

"I went to Coalinga Junior College in California for a year and got my grades up to the college level. I had a real good year at Coalinga and made quarterback on the All-America junior college team."

Willie Wood streaks downfield after intercepting a Colt pass.

A close friend of Willie's was attending Southern Cal, where they were in the process of rebuilding their football team under a new coach, Don Clark. So Willie decided to go there. He alternated at quarterback in his sophomore year under Clark's system of rotating talent. By his junior year, Willie was on the number one unit. Late in his junior year, however, he suffered a shoulder separation.

During his senior year, Wood saw only limited action because of the shoulder injury. He was used primarily on defense and attracted little attention among the pros.

"Just before the pro draft, I heard through the grapevine that they thought I was too brittle to play pro ball," Willie later explained. "I didn't know what to do because I wanted so much to play pro ball.

"Bill Butler, one of my coaches back in the old Boys' Club days had followed my career, so I went to him for advice. He suggested that I write to all the pro teams. They sent me back questionnaires to fill out, but I only heard directly from one team.

"That was Green Bay. They were in Los Angeles to play the Rams late in the season. Jack Vanisi, who used to be the Packers' business manager, called me up and asked if I wanted to play with them. Naturally I told him yes. They said I would get a contract and I did."

As a free agent on a championship-minded club like Green Bay, Wood knew he had a tough battle on his hands if he hoped to make the club. The first year (1960) was rough. He didn't know what to expect when he went to camp. A good many of the other rookies had played in the All-Star game in Chicago but he hadn't. The only bowl game Willie had ever played in was the Copper Bowl in Phoenix. There weren't many jobs open, and he felt his chances were slimmer because he was a free agent.

The Packers had drafted eleven defensive backs that year but, in the end, Dick Pesonen and Willie Wood were the only two who made it.

Wood didn't get much chance to play as a rookie, but he did blossom out as a punt-return expert. This is one of the most difficult jobs in pro football, because the receiver is fair game for those big men charging down the field. And Willie is only five-feet-ten, and he weighs just 188 pounds.

By the time the 1961 season started, Willie had moved into the starting lineup as a replacement for Emlen Tunnell, who was close to retirement. But it had been an uphill fight.

In his rookie year, Wood was called upon to fill in for Jesse Whittenton at one of the defensive halfback jobs in a game against Baltimore. Johnny Unitas, an expert against all defenses, decided to single out the rookie for special attention. Unitas connected with Raymond Berry for two touchdown passes right over Willie's head. Wood thought his professional football career was over.

"Those were the worst mistakes I ever made," he said. "I figured my boo-boos lost the game [Baltimore won, 38–24]. After the game Norb Hecker, our defensive coach, told me to forget it. He said those things happen to everybody.

"When the '61 season started I figured I was the number six defensive back, and we carried only six. There were some good rookies looking for jobs, too. Tunnell was getting old and we needed somebody to step in. Dale Hackbart got the first shot, but finally they gave it to me."

Tunnell had talked defense to Wood constantly. He recognized a kindred soul in Willie, who had written a letter asking for a job. Many years earlier, Emlen had walked into the New York Giants' office, uninvited, to ask for a trial.

Under the veteran player's coaching, Wood developed into the same type of teeth-rattling tackler as Tunnell. And he even improved on his punt-return work. Hecker, who had been one of his boosters from the start, commented, "Willie

Trying to block a field goal,
Willie (24) leaps high into the air.

can play a man loose, which tempts the quarterback to throw the ball. Once the ball is in the air, he reacts quickly and goes after it."

Despite Willie's size he can jump like John Thomas and can tap the cross bar with his wrist. Mike Ditka, the man-tank of the Chicago Bears, once said that Willie hit him harder than he ever had been hit before.

While he was on the 1961 championship team that humbled the New York Giants in the title game, 37–0, Willie led the league in punt returns with an average of 16.1 yards. The following year with another NFL championship team, he led the league with nine interceptions.

Although Willie has returned a total of 91 kicks for 1,025 yards in his NFL career, he thinks the art is fading.

"We used to call the punt return a fifth down because a good runback would give the offense a better chance of scoring," said Wood. "But it's getting tougher. They are punting the ball higher to let those defensive men get down under it.

"Everybody works on the special kicking units now. We have a good book on all the punters. Fellows like Yale Lary of Detroit and Bobby Joe Green of the Bears still boot them high and far. Some of the others are working more on just getting the ball up in the air to prevent any return. I have to make more fair catches now because of the high punts."

Most of the teams in the NFL try to kick the ball away from Willie on a punt situation. It doesn't always work, though. In 1964 the Chicago Bears couldn't get him out of their hair. Willie returned one Bear punt 64 yards to set up the first touchdown in a game at Wrigley Field. He brought back another kick 42 yards to set up the second touchdown. Then he intercepted a pass to start a drive that ended with a Green Bay field goal. Willie also fumbled, a misplay that set up the Bears' field goal so he had a hand in all the scoring in Green Bay's 17–3 victory.

"The punt returns by Wood were the key plays," said George Halas, coach of the Bears. "We were doing a good job, holding them off in the first half. Then one play killed us—the punt. After the ball bounced, our men stopped and away went Willie. On the second punt at least three of our men had a clean shot at him but they all missed."

Even Willie had to be satisfied with himself after that effort when Hank Gremminger awarded him the game ball.

"That's the first one I ever got," said Wood. "I guess that is just about the biggest day I ever had.

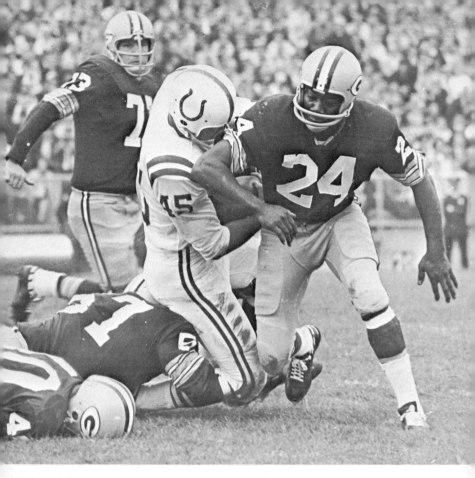

Wood (24) blocks Colt halfback Lenny Lyles
in the game that resulted in Willie's winning the game ball.

The boys were blocking awfully hard for me. They kept telling me, 'We'll block and you run.' What was a fellow going to do but run when those big men tell you that?"

It might seem that Wood would have ambitions about returning to his old quarterback job, the position he played until he joined the pros. He doesn't, though. He admitted that at first he missed it. Then he began to realize that perhaps he wouldn't have been good enough to succeed on offense. He has adjusted to defense and likes it. In fact, he has no desire at all to play on offense any more. Safety suits him fine.

Perhaps Vince Lombardi, his boss, summed up Willie Wood's story best when he said:

"We spend over fifty thousand dollars a year to scout all the colleges, and then we get Willie through a letter he mailed with a four-cent stamp."

After the Packers won the 1962 championship from the Giants, the Green Bay fans showed their affection for Willie Wood.

Willie is no four-cent player, though. He commands a fine salary as befits a talented regular on one of the great teams of the National Football League. He could use his name for any number of lucrative positions during the off season. But it is to Willie Wood's credit that he prefers to work with kids when not playing football. In 1961 and 1962 he taught social adjustment at Elliott Junior High School and Hart Junior High School in Washington. In 1963 he accepted an appointment in the District of Columbia Recreation Department with the title of Roving Leader.

"They found out that their regular program was not reaching a number of kids," said Willie. "Some boys are just not athletically inclined. Some have other interests. In many cases, there are family problems that bother kids.

"The Department decided to set up Roving Leaders in various areas of the District. Our job is to direct certain individuals who have problems. We work as counselors in getting them jobs. We act as a go-between for kids with a problem and for kids who are having troubles at home.

"When we come across a boy who is a school drop-out, we try to revert his interests to the educational program. . . . I try to gain the confidence of the kids and direct their misused energy to something constructive.

"Sometimes it doesn't work, of course, but eighty-five to ninety per cent of the time it does work. We have gangs like the Decatur Street gang, the Uptowners, the Downtowners, the 12th Street Boys. We don't try to break them up but attempt to direct their interest to something else.

"I can look at some of my boys and see myself a few years back. Our problems were similar to theirs. We didn't know which way to go. We had our own little groups and our own little fights. They were typical of the area, a poverty area."

When Willie finishes his pro football career, he wants to devote his life to this problem. He feels that the personal satisfactions are great even though he knows he could make more money doing something else.

Willie Wood has come a long way since his days of standing around on street corners, and he would like to help others to achieve higher goals. "I like to think," he has said, "that I could be like Jabbo Kenner. He's never too busy to help somebody else. He's done a wonderful job in something he wanted to do. What could be better than that."

If Willie succeeds in this aim, he will be a hero in more than the NFL.

Tommy McDonald

9

Tommy McDonald bubbles with energy. Shake a bottle of pop with your thumb over the top. Then let it go. *Whoosh!* That's the way Tommy lives.

Pro football players don't usually make swan dives into towel hampers. They don't leap into the arms of a quarterback after catching a touchdown. But Tommy McDonald does.

When Norm "The Dutchman" Van Brocklin left the Philadelphia Eagles to become head coach of the Minnesota Vikings, impish Tommy told Norm's replacement, Sonny Jurgensen, "Don't worry, Sonny, I'll make you as great a passer as The Dutchman."

They tell stories about the day in the Eagles'

training camp at Hershey, Pennsylvania, when Tommy dangled from a third floor balcony, holding on with one hand. And there is the time he is supposed to have climbed on the roof of Jurgensen's station wagon as it rolled past startled spectators in surburban Philadelphia. The Eagles also still talk about his dying-swan leap over their heads into the middle of a group posing for a team picture after the 1960 championship season.

Tommy was the unpredictable zany of the Eagles' basketball team that used to tour the Pennsylvania-New Jersey-Delaware area in the off season. He would climb on a teammate's shoulders to dunk a basket, a maneuver straight out of the tricks of the Harlem Globetrotters. A few minutes later he might dash into the bleachers, bounce among the customers and then dribble in to shoot a basket. Once he came out on the floor in a pair of old-fashioned orange bloomers.

Unable to restrain his enthusiasm over a key interception by big John Baker, he once catapulted his five-foot-nine-and-a-half inch 170-pound frame off the Eagles' bench and carried the six-foot-six, 260-pound defensive end in triumph from the end zone to the bench.

Tommy McDonald has dedicated himself to proving that there is a place for a runt in profes-

Tommy McDonald

sional football. With Eddie LeBaron in retirement, Tommy is one of the smallest regulars in the National Football League. On a field covered with big men like Jim Parker, Doug Atkins, Roger Brown and Rosey Grier, Tommy stands out like a wire-haired terrier in a pack of great danes.

He was always smaller than the other boys. In fact, he says he weighed only four pounds, eight ounces at birth. His father always wanted Tommy to be a professional baseball player because he had been a pretty fair pitcher in his day. As a boy on a small farm near the tiny town of Roy, New Mexico, Tommy practiced baseball, basketball and football and ran a mile to school every day.

In the hope that he would grow a little more before entering high school, Tommy's parents had him spend an extra year in the eighth grade. He didn't grow much, but he did get a motorbike as a consolation prize. Later, an accident on that same motorbike cost him the tip of his left thumb.

When the family moved to Albuquerque, New Mexico, Tommy became a star athlete at Highland High School. In his senior year he broke scoring records in football and basketball and won a number of medals in the dashes and hurdle races at the state track meet.

The universities of New Mexico and Southern

Methodist offered football scholarships to the pride of the McDonald family, but he wound up at Oklahoma, almost by accident. Bruce Drake, the Oklahoma basketball coach, saw Tommy perform in a track meet and also in an all-star football game. He passed the word along to people at Norman, Oklahoma. Soon Pop Ivy, an assistant at Oklahoma, invited Tommy to the campus. By that time, young McDonald was almost five feet, six inches tall and weighed close to 145 pounds.

At Oklahoma Tommy first met Bud Wilkinson, who was to have a profound influence on his life. In fact, there still is a fine personal relationship between the former All-America halfback and the man who coached the Sooners to two national championships and a 47-game winning streak. But Bud Wilkinson is still *Mr.* Wilkinson to Tommy McDonald.

While he was playing at Oklahoma, Tommy was a running halfback in Wilkinson's split-T style of offense. The Oklahoma system was based on quick-opening plays in which the linemen would just brush an opponent with a block. A covey of fleet backs would burst through the holes quickly before they could be closed up.

As a running halfback, McDonald often was called upon to take the ball, fake a run, and then throw a pass when he was about to be tackled. In football language this is known as the option play, in which the back has the choice of running with the ball or throwing a forward pass. Tommy completed 17 out of 24 in one year and 16 out of 21 the following season.

In his senior year, 1956, Tommy blossomed out as a pass receiver. Jimmy Harris, who ironically was to become a defensive back in the professional ranks, would throw the ball as far as he could and Tommy would run downfield with breakneck speed and grab it.

Because of his size, Tommy had not given much thought to a career in pro ball. But a view of Doak Walker as a flanker in a game carried on television started Tommy thinking about the pros. Walker was taller than McDonald, but he was no giant. If Walker could make it as a pass catcher, why not McDonald?

The Eagles must have had one of the most successful drafts in the history of pro ball when they picked the 1956 stars for 1957 delivery. Philadelphia had finished last in the NFL and, consequently, had the first pick in the draft.

Clarence Peaks was number one; Billy Barnes, number two; McDonald number three; Sonny

Coach Bud Wilkinson and the 1956 Oklahoma team
celebrate their victory over Maryland in the Orange Bowl.

Jurgensen number four, and Jimmy Harris was
number five. All of them made good in the NFL.

The Eagles had been a bit dubious about select-
ing McDonald because of his size. Vince McNally,
the general manager of the club, asked Wilkinson
for his opinion before wasting a choice on Tommy.

"I don't think Tommy is big enough to make it
as a running back," said Wilkinson. "But I think
he will make an excellent flanker."

Shortly after the draft, the Eagles discovered that they had picked something more than just another football player. Tommy had come to Philadelphia in January, 1957, to receive the Maxwell Award as the outstanding college football player after being named to the All-America team for the second time. On the day of the banquet, Tommy went to the airlines office to check his return flight to Oklahoma.

Unknown to Tommy, the airline clerks and all girl employees in the area had been alerted to be on the lookout for a stick-up man known as the

The Eagles' number three draft choice, Tommy McDonald, poses with Coach Hugh Devore (left) and General Manager Vince McNally.

"Lonely Hearts Bandit." Tommy bore a marked resemblance to a pencil sketch of the bandit that had been distributed to all offices in the downtown area of Philadelphia.

When Tommy walked into reconfirm his ticket, a girl took one look and pushed a buzzer that was connected with police headquarters. Before Tommy could finish his business, two burly detectives grabbed him and started searching him. Naturally, Tommy did not know who they were or what they wanted. He fought back.

Before the action became too heated, Tommy asked the girl to check with the Eagles' office. McNally rushed to the airlines and identified his future star. Everybody apologized profusely.

"I was just about to belt you," said Tommy.

"It's a good thing you didn't," said a detective who had been in the back of the room. "We were sure you were the right guy, and I had a .45 trained right at your stomach."

Tommy didn't exactly tear the league apart in his rookie year. In fact, he and Jimmy Brown sat on the bench during most of the 1957 College All-Star game at Chicago, while Curly Lambeau experimented with Jon Arnett and Billy Barnes against the New York Giants.

When Tommy arrived at training camp after

that experience, he was not even sure he would survive the cuts. Hughie Devore, then coach of the Eagles, kept him on the squad, but he wasn't playing. Billy Barnes of Wake Forest, another rookie, had won the running back job. McDonald was used primarily on punt and kickoff returns.

Tommy didn't really get a chance to show his stuff until Bill Stribling, an offensive end, was injured. The Eagles were playing the Redskins and Devore started McDonald at right end. He scored twice, the first on a brilliant leaping catch between two defenders which completed a 62-yard play. Bert Bell, the late commissioner of the NFL, was so impressed he called it "one of the greatest catches I've ever seen."

Buck Shaw took over from Devore in 1958, and Dutch Van Brocklin became the Eagles' quarterback. The new order was perfect for McDonald. Shaw installed him at the right halfback or flankerback position, where he was destined to become one of the great pass-catching stars in NFL history. The right half, or flanker, job is primarily a position for a pass catcher. In the pro ranks, the left half position is normally the job of a powerful running back who alternates with the fullback.

Van Brocklin could throw the long bomb and McDonald could catch it. The combination be-

came one of the most feared in the league. As
Tommy said later, after the Dutchman had become coach of the Vikings, "Van Brocklin taught
me almost everything I know about pass receiving."

It was Van Brocklin who told Tommy to change
speeds—not to blast off with everything he had,
but to stop and go, maneuver and feint and then
cut loose when he finally got behind his defensive
man.

McDonald suffered one of the few serious injuries of his career early in the 1959 season in a
game with the San Francisco Forty-Niners. Slicing
across the middle in dangerous territory, where a
receiver is vulnerable to both the linebacker and
the defensive back, McDonald was hit by a pair of
old Oklahoma buddies, linebacker Jerry Tubbs
and back Dave Baker. The result was a broken
jaw.

Two weeks later, playing against the New York
Giants in Philadelphia, Tommy scored four touchdowns, despite another crack on the jaw.

Although the hairline fracture forced Tommy
to sip his meals through a straw for the rest of the
season, he finished with 47 catches for 10 touchdowns and placed second only to Raymond Berry
of Baltimore among NFL pass receivers.

In 1959, for the first time since the glory years of 1947–48–49, the Eagles had really been in the race. They finished in a tie for second place in the Eastern Conference.

McDonald and Van Brocklin pooled their talents with a fine Eagle squad in 1960 and Philadelphia finished with a 10–2 record, the best in either conference.

In the championship game against Green Bay, the Dutchman hit Tommy with a 22-yard pass and then came right back with a 35-yard gainer on the next play for the first Eagle touchdown in a 17–13 upset win over the Packers.

Although Tommy and the Eagles mourned the departure of Norman Van Brocklin, who left to become coach of the Vikings, Sonny Jurgensen proved to be a most capable replacement at quarterback. In 1961 McDonald had his best year, catching 64 passes for a league-leading total of 1,114 yards. He also matched his 1960 total of 13 touchdown passes.

Tommy always gave advice in the huddle. It usually was designed to get the ball thrown in his direction.

"I can beat this guy—easy," Tommy would tell Jurgensen. "Throw it to me."

When a newsman asked Jurgensen who called a

Eagle quarterback Sonny Jurgensen (9) laughs with his favorite pass receiver, Tommy McDonald, after a tight game with the Redskins in 1961. The two completed a pass in the last 16 seconds of play.

play that had won a game for the Eagles, the former Duke quarterback replied, "McDonald called the play. Of course, he called a play every time he came into the huddle. And, funny thing, they all were passes to McDonald."

Although Tommy caught 56 passes in 1962 and 41 in 1963, the Eagles finished last in the Eastern Conference two years in a row. A change in ownership was followed by a change in coaches, with Joe Kuharich succeeding Nick Skorich. Both McDonald and Jurgensen were traded to other clubs.

At first Tommy talked of retirement and hinted he would not report to the Dallas Cowboys because of his many off-the-field business interests in Philadelphia.

"I just couldn't believe it had happened," said McDonald. "I feel as if I've been thrown away like an old shoe."

Tommy soon changed his mind and reported to the Cowboys. He had a few problems working into the offense used by Tom Landry at Dallas. He didn't score his first touchdown until after midseason. After Tommy caught Don Meredith's pass and scrambled 48 yards to score against the Giants at Yankee Stadium, he leaped into Meredith's arms.

"Hardest lick I got all day," said Meredith after the winning game.

A number of Philadelphia newsmen had made the trip to New York to see Tommy, and there was a knot of reporters around his locker after the game. Tommy didn't let them down.

"The boys were beginning to kid me," he said. "They were calling me snake-bite boy. As soon as I caught a ball, the officials would throw down three or four flags and the team would march backward 15 yards on a penalty. I didn't even score in the pre-season games, so I was 0 for 13 going into this one. You might say I was overdue."

Tommy finished the 1964 season with only two touchdown passes, a career low. But he did grab 46 passes in a year when he was used largely as a decoy for Frank Clarke.

Anyone who sees Tommy McDonald play football is watching an accomplished artist. He can play-act like the best actor on Broadway. He'll put on a deadpan face with a blank stare, suggesting he couldn't care less about the next play because he isn't involved. Then, when the fans relax, expecting the halfback to run, McDonald will suddenly be sifting through the defense, feinting with his head and body until he shakes loose. And then away he goes.

Boys who think they have to be six-feet-five, like Green Bay's Boyd Dowler, or a burly six-feet-three, like the Bears' 230-pound Mike Ditka, can take heart in the story of Tommy McDonald.

They said he was "too small" and would "never make it." But Tommy fooled them all. As his old coach Buck Shaw once said:

"Give me a squad of Tommy McDonalds, and I'll win every game."

Lenny Moore

10

Lenny Moore walked slowly through the gathering darkness on his way from the training table in the cafeteria to the dormitory. It was a sweltering August night on the campus of Western Maryland College in Westminster, Maryland, where the Baltimore Colts were encamped for their 1964 training season.

On the pavement some of the other Colts were joking and engaging in the rough horseplay of athletes with time on their hands. But Lenny walked past them without a word and climbed the stone steps quietly. He was deadly serious as he settled down in a chair in a conference room on the main floor of the Dormitory, for a visiting sports writer was waiting there to interview him.

Sports writers had not been bothering Lenny very much during the past two seasons. The speedy halfback, who had been nicknamed "Sputnik" by the late "Big Daddy" Lipscomb, had been sputtering for two years. There had been rumors that he had been offered around the league as trading material. But it seemed nobody was interested. The experts were whispering that Lenny Moore was "all washed up."

It seemed unthinkable to Moore that he could be all finished at the age of thirty. Hadn't he scored more touchdowns than any other Colt in the history of the club? Didn't he still have the talent that had made Rip Engle, his college coach at Penn State, say, "Lenny is the most exciting back I've ever seen"?

"What has happened to you, Lenny?" the sports writer asked. "Why are you only the number two left halfback in this camp? Do you know that some of the boys are saying you are only as good as you want to be?"

Moore had heard this talk for two years. He ran his finger around the open neck of his sports shirt

Lenny Moore.

as he pondered his answers.

"I've heard all this and more, too," Lenny said slowly. "I don't even want to talk about it because I have decided that the only way I can kill off talk like that is by going out on the field and having a big year.

"For the first time in three years I'm healthy. I'm physically sound and that is the big difference. Nobody knows how a man feels except himself. If a man is hurt a little here and there, you can't expect him to give one hundred per cent. But sometimes in this league you have to give one hundred and ten per cent."

The "little" injuries Moore talked about were actually major problems. In 1961 he had suffered a head injury. In the last pre-season exhibition game of 1962, he had suffered a broken kneecap when knocked out of bounds on a bruising double tackle by Pittsburgh's Brady Keys and Dick Haley. In 1963 he suffered damaged ribs, then an emergency appendectomy that forced him to miss two regular-season games. Later in the year he was kicked on the head. Dizzy spells kept him out of the lineup for the last five games of the season.

"I want to prove to myself that I still have it," Lenny told the reporter. "I want to shut up a lot of mouths that have been saying I'm finished. . . .

Washed up? Why, I feel just like I did when I broke in with the Colts in 1956 and when we won the league championship in 1958 and 1959.

"I keep hearing talk that I am trade bait. It bothers me for only one reason. I know it's false. I had a long talk with Carroll Rosenbloom [the Colts' owner], Don Kellett [their general manager] and Coach Don Shula. They told me there was nothing to it.

"There was a big rumor that I didn't want to play in Baltimore and that I was dissatisfied with the front office. That's all wrong. I own a house in Baltimore. I'm in love with the town. I want to stay there and do a job for the team and for myself."

Then the writer asked Moore about being the number two left halfback.

"That is only the way it should be," Moore replied. "Tom Matte did a fine job for us last year when I was hurt. It is only natural that I should be behind him right now. It is up to me to work my way back and take the job away from Tom."

It is history now that Moore did fight his way back, did take the job away from Tom Matte. At the end of the 1964 season, Lenny had scored 20 touchdowns, a National Football League record, and he led the NFL in scoring with a total of 120 points. Less than six months after that sultry night of the interview in Westminster, Moore was taking bows as the winner of the "Comeback of the Year" award in the league.

"Man, that's nice," commented Lenny. "Particularly when things looked so shaky. I had been out of commission for most of two years, and when you're getting older, you wonder about your ability to come back."

Things really had looked shaky for Lenny. He hadn't told the reporter the whole story at Westminster. He had not told him what really happened when he walked into the Colts' office for that June conference with Rosenbloom, Kellett and Shula.

Kellett had been offering Lenny around the league. A deal had been discussed with New York before the Giants traded Sam Huff to Washington. The Redskins had been sounded out. So had Detroit, Los Angeles and Green Bay.

All of the clubs contacted had expressed the same reaction. They told Kellett they thought Lenny had "goofed off" the year before and probably would no longer be able to play hard for a full season because of his series of injuries. The Colts had finally not traded Moore for the simple reason that nobody wanted to give up top-flight material for him.

When Moore asked for a conference with the club's front office, they all talked very frankly to one another. Coach Shula asked Moore point-blank about the reports that he was not satisfied to play in Baltimore. Shula had been very disappointed with Moore's playing in 1963, Shula's first season as head coach after succeeding Weeb Ewbank.

Moore protested that he wanted to stay with the Colts. He was confident that he could come back with a big year. He didn't want to be traded.

"That's what I wanted to hear," said Shula. "Okay, you stay with the club. But let's get it straight right now. You open the season behind Tom Matte. It's up to you to prove you can win back the job."

Despite a fine training season, Lenny was still the number two boy behind Matte when the season started at Bloomington, Minnesota. The Vikings manhandled the Colts and rolled up a shocking total of 488 yards in a 34–24 victory. Moore got into the game, scored twice and led Baltimore with 26 yards but the Colts were badly beaten.

After that defeat Baltimore's next stop was another road game. This time it was at Green Bay

Coach Don Shula, the man who was willing
to give Lenny Moore a second chance.

against the Packers. With Paul Hornung back in the lineup, the Packers were favored to win the Western Conference, especially after their opening-day success against the Chicago Bears.

Shula started Moore against the Packers in a game the Colts had to win. Midway in the first quarter, Johnny Unitas sent Lenny swinging out to the right side. The Packers had the blitz on. Two men rushed at Unitas, leaving Dan Currie, the left linebacker, to handle Moore.

That was all Moore needed: one-on-one, with long-legged speedy Lenny against a sturdy linebacker. Lenny faked toward the middle of the field and then cut back down the right sideline. Currie wasn't within 10 yards of him when Moore caught Unitas' pass and went on for the first touchdown of the game on a 52-yard scoring play.

In the clubhouse after the game, Lenny talked about the incident. "I told myself, 'Please don't drop this one. Watch, yourself. You've got to catch this one!'"

The Packers came back and tied the score before Moore broke loose again, this time with a smashing 4-yard run on a trap play. Lenny carried Ray Nitschke, Green Bay's all-league middle linebacker, into the end zone with him.

"He ran as if he wanted it," said Nitschke.

And that was the story of Moore in 1964. He always ran as if he wanted it.

In the second crucial game with the Packers, at Baltimore's Memorial Stadium on October 18, the 190-pound back from Reading, Pennsylvania, convinced everybody in the park that he was the Lenny Moore of old. Taking a quick pitch from Unitas on the Packers' 20, Lenny hit the left side of the huge Green Bay line, slithering away from tacklers on the way. Henry Jordan had his hands on him but couldn't hold him. Hank Gremminger also had a piece of him. Jesse Whittenon, the last man between Lenny and the goal line, tried to flag him down. All he got for his efforts was a piggy-back ride as far as the 2-yard-line before Moore shook him off and went in for the six-pointer.

Later in the same game, Lenny again drove off that left side for five yards and the winning touchdown of a 24–21 game.

The touchdowns were important but, even more important, was the way they had been scored. In the years since 1956, when he had joined the Colts out of Penn State, most of Lenny's runs had been of the open-field variety. He had dazzled defenders with his quick feints and blinding speed. But the 1964 runs against the Packers were different. They were power runs of the type that a Jimmy

Brown would be proud to make.

Lenny's line-smashing efforts vindicated Shula and his predecessor, Weeb Ewbank, who had been roundly criticized for moving Moore from the wide flanker position to the tight halfback job. As a flanker who lined up outside the end in the pros' typical three-end offense, Moore did not have to blast away against the 270-pound defensive men who man the interior of NFL lines. On the outside he usually was pitted against a slender, speedy defensive back. But while running from the tight halfback position, Lenny actually became a second fullback, whose main job was carrying the ball and not catching passes.

Gino Marchetti, the veteran defensive end who came out of retirement to help the Colts win the Western Conference title in 1964, was lavish in his praise of Moore after that second Green Bay game.

"I never saw anybody run like that against the Packers," said Marchetti who, with other Colts, had been critical of Lenny's failure to do better in 1962 and 1963.

When Ewbank first decided to move Moore to the inside running job in 1962, Lenny had not been too happy. "I like to pit myself against a great defensive back and see what I can do," said Moore. "If you're a professional, I think you have to feel that way. But if they want me to play inside, that is where I'll play. I was a flanker for years and fell in love with it. But I am thankful they think I can play more than one position."

Fans flooded Baltimore newspapers with letters complaining that Ewbank was playing Moore out of position and wasting his great talents as a speedy pass catcher by playing him in the running back position. When Ewbank left and Shula replaced him, it was assumed that the new coach would move Lenny back to the flank. But Shula did nothing of the kind. He left Moore at the inside position.

"When I took over I studied the films of the Colts' games," said Shula. "I needed a back who could run and be a good pass receiver, too. Lenny can do both things. In fact, he is the best running back we have. So I think it would be wasting talent to put him outside where he never would run with the ball."

There were very few critics of Shula's decision while the Colts were manhandling the Western Conference opposition in 1964. Baltimore sports editors reported a sharp decline in letters to the editor from irate football fans.

The statistics certainly backed up Shula. Lenny carried the ball 157 times and gained 584 yards.

He also caught 21 passes for 472 yards for a total gain of 1,046 yards.

Even more startling are the figures on average yardage gained by rushing. Although the great Jim Brown of Cleveland usually leads the league in rushing, with well over 1,000 yards, his average carry is 5.2 yards during his pro career. Lenny

Lenny Moore gains yardage against Green Bay.

Moore's average is 5.26 per carry for nine years in the big time.

No wonder a veteran defensive back like Ben Scotti, who played with several teams, made this comment:

"Lenny is the toughest target in the league. He drops his shoulder and bobs and weaves and doesn't give you more to shoot at. When you try to hit him you only get one-half of what you thought you were going to get."

Gary Kerkorian, a sub quarterback of a few years back, summed up Moore's ability in these words:

"I never have seen a ball carrier get into so much trouble and then get out of so much trouble."

Moore, born on November 25, 1933 in Reading, Pennsylvania, had to come up the hard way as one of a family of eight children. But at Reading High School he scored 23 touchdowns in his senior year. Andy Stopper, his high-school coach, said, "Lenny was so good that when you tried to tell people about him, they thought you were lying."

Rip Engle once analyzed Moore's talent at Penn State in this capsule comment: "He's like mercury. Instead of running he flows. He always knows where to turn, when to hit into the hole and when to hold back and wait for his chance at an opening."

When the Colts' officials were trying to make up their minds about their number one draft choice in 1956, a scout was sent to Penn State to check information on Lenny with Joe Paterno, the Nittany Lions' backfield coach.

Paterno sent back the word, "Tell the Colts not to miss him. If they do, it will be the greatest mistake they could make."

No wonder the professional scouting report on Lenny before the 1964 championship game read like this:

"The best combination runner-receiver in pro football. He has the speed to run a deep pass pattern from the halfback position. Don't let him get loose in a one-on-one situation with a linebacker or he will kill you."

When they started passing out awards to the "New Lenny Moore" after the 1964 season, he told Cameron Snyder of the Baltimore *Sun:*

"The Man Upstairs was looking out for me— and the blocking was good, too."

Index

(Photograph entries appear in italics)

THE PUNT PASS AND KICK LIBRARY

N.F.L.